D0501509

IF LOVE IS THE ANSWER, WHAT IS THE QUESTION?

Uta West

IF LOVE IS THE ANSWER, WHAT IS THE QUESTION?

Uta West

McGRAW-HILL BOOK COMPANY
New York   St. Louis   San Francisco
Düsseldorf   Mexico   Panama   Toronto

OKANAGAN REGIONAL LIBRARY

717086

Book design by Elaine Gongora.

Copyright © 1977 by Uta West.
All rights reserved. Printed in the United States of America. No part
of this publication may be reproduced, stored in a retrieval system,
or transmitted, in any form or by any means, electronic, mechanical,
photocopying, recording, or otherwise, without the prior permission of
the publisher.

1 2 3 4 5 6 7 8 9 B P B P 7 9 8 7

Library of Congress Cataloging in Publication Data

West, Uta.
If love is the answer, what is the question?

Bibliography: p.
1. Interpersonal relations.   2. Love.
3. Friendship.   4. Sex.   I. Title.
HM132.W385   301.41   76–50661
ISBN 0–07–069476–1

"(You Make Me Feel Like) A Natural Woman"
Words & Music by Carole King, Gerry Goffin & Jerry Wexler.
© Copyright 1967 by Screen Gems–EMI Music Inc.
All rights reserved. Used by permission.

This book is for
Marlene and Marvin,
who are alive in these pages,
speaking out with their
customary candor and wit,
as they remain
ever alive in my memory

Acknowledgments

I wish to thank Elaine Markson, for her faith, and my editor Joyce Johnson, for the care and effort she expended, and, especially, I thank the many anonymous contributors who have shared with me their thoughts and experiences.

Live the questions now.
Perhaps you will then... live
along some distant day
into the answer.

–Rainer Maria Rilke
Letters to a Young Poet

Contents

Introduction

Once a young man who was leaving the country the next day tried to persuade me to go to bed with him for the night. "We are here together, talking to each other—we are having a *relationship*," he insisted, but would have bitten off his tongue before he said "love." Whatever else may or may not be implied, there is no doubt that love refers to a quality of feeling—and of *strong* feeling, at that.

Having established this emotional context, however, we may be hard put to discover the other common denominators. When people say, "I love ice cream," are they talking about an intensified form of the word "like," or is what's implied here a *passion* for ice cream, something that might conceivably get out of control? Certainly, both possibilities must be considered.

Consider further, if you will, the curious fact that people will say "love" very freely when referring to food, or music, or their pets, but are extremely cautious and hesitant about using that word with regard to people. "Relationship," on the other hand, is an O.K. word, according to our unwritten cultural code; it smacks of school and the psychiatrist's office, reassuring us with its blandness and respectability ("Discuss the relationship between the industrial revolution and the literature of alienation." "Your dependency is characteristic of your relationship with your mother." Etc.).

A woman I know told me that some years ago she'd been seeing a young man who called to say he had something important to tell her. All excited and expectant, she awaited the great revelation, and here's what he said: "You know, I really *like* you very much." He couldn't possibly have said "love" because to him it would have meant a firm commitment to marriage. More recently, a highly sophisticated man said that during moments of passion, the words "I love you" come naturally to his lips. However, he felt he had to stop himself from saying them because the woman usually assumed the words implied a promise for the future, instead of expressing the way he felt at that particular moment.

Why, then, be so foolhardy as to write about love at all? Aside from my personal need to make some sense out of the confusion, the subject of love seems to be of greater concern than ever to people today. You hear lots of talk about why "relationships" aren't working. Endless stories—indignant, sad, funny—about the myriad ways they're going down the drain, endless discussions about how things *ought* to be, how to make love conform to our specifications.

You would think there were no other problems in the world, no recession or depression, no injustice or ecological disaster looming on the horizon. Have we really become so callous and self-involved? Or is it rather a profound sense of helplessness that makes us shun the larger issues we no longer feel able to fight or control and turn to the cultivation of our personal gardens, where some kind of salvage still seems possible?

It is a general rule that family bonds grow stronger in times of social and cultural upheaval; during wars and economic stress there are more marriages, more babies, more intense love affairs, and more exotic experimentation with sex. The need for emotional warmth and private satisfactions to offset the grim realities of the outside world seems to be at the root of these seemingly selfish preoccupations. But now there is this difficulty: family bonds, marriage and babies, love affairs, and even sex, are no longer the refuge and the consolation they used to be. They have become as problematic as everything else—if not more so.

We are appalled at the wreckage we encounter. Much too late and too slowly, it seemed, we began to question some of the myths and assumptions that had deadened and constricted human intercourse. All we really had in mind was reform—a little cleanup and alteration—but as soon as we started to tinker with it, the whole structure came apart. To our amazement and horror, these myths turned out to be the supporting pillars of a complex system upon which depended our most intimate associations. Obviously, the structure was rotten and had to go. But now we do not know how to rebuild —our changed and changing needs are too many and too contradictory. Not that we lack blueprints and models—hardly a day goes by but that someone publishes a how-to book guaranteed to solve all our problems. But too many blueprints amounts to the same thing as having none, and in the meantime we are without emotional shelter, at a time when we need it most.

Most of the new theories and programs are actually much the same as the old ones—but dressed in mod clothes, so to speak. Our legacy of myth persists in somewhat altered forms. We may be skeptical about the phrase "God is love" yet spend our lives in worshipful pursuit of the "meaningful relationship." The puritan ethic lives on in popular psychology, in the form of "working" on marriage and the new performance-oriented sexuality.

If time and time again we fail to find fulfillment, our faith in the magical efficacy of love is not shaken. We blame our shortcomings, or those of our partners, the time, the place, or the circumstances. Rarely does it occur to us to question the very premises upon which our search is built . . . to wonder if it might not be the way we've been programed to think about love that needs to be re-examined. For as any computer can tell you, to get the right answer you must first of all ask the right question.

We like to believe that when people get together what happens between them is a personal and individual matter. But now that there are no more ground rules—now that we can no longer even rebel, because there is no accepted code to rebel *against*—we can see with increasing clarity how much of our most intimate experience is predicated on an internalized climate of views that seems not only natural and inevitable but universal. For myth is not dependent on reason, or experience. It is a function of desire; when myth claims things are a certain way, it means we wish—we *demand*—that they be this way.

But myths get tired and old and worn-out, and must be periodically renewed if they are to serve as creative rather than destructive forces. Ordinarily, this is a gradual process, allowing plenty of time for adjustment. But in our speeded-up times, the myth-wrecking crews came and went before we even knew what hit us. Other myths were hastily thrown into the gap, but these makeshift constructs provide no real shelter. In fact, they tend to be more dangerous than the old ones (if they are not the old ones in disguise), for they lack a firm foundation in human nature; they have not been tried and tested, not been found adequate to our needs.

I think it is necessary to admit the confusion, to be honest and courageous enough to accept the fact that there are no more sheltering beliefs, and that for the time being we must live in the open. Otherwise we cannot even begin to untangle the snarls and shall merely succumb to despair—the what's-the-use? attitude which has, among other effects, produced a virtual stalemate in the relations between the sexes.

The search for connectedness takes several primary forms. Though I deal with them separately, it must be understood that all such categories are artificial and are used only for purposes of clarification. In reality, the different kinds of love interweave and overlap. I look first into romantic love, glorified in our culture to the point of idolatry, and often talked and sung about as if it were the only love worthy of the name. This is the kind of love we are said to "fall" into.

Women's liberation has begun to confirm what we have long known or suspected: that living through and for husband, children, and family is not necessarily the highroad to happiness. But the women's movement has made hardly any inroads into the concept of romanticism. The notion that women may be more likely to find love-and-happiness in lesbianism does nothing to alter the mythology of romance, with its emphasis on the special thrill of instant attraction, the justification of suffering as the "price" of love, and the extraordinary weight we place on such emotionally wrenching liaisons.

It is the modern, independent, would-be liberated woman who is especially victimized by the myths surrounding romantic love. For while her life and her goals have changed dramatically, she is tied to archaic dreams and desires; she continues to harbor emotional needs and expectations that preclude her being open and imaginative in her amorous encounters. The result is a gap—between beliefs and behavior, between public stance and private necessities—that manifests itself in a number of curious and ironic ways. This gap cannot be bridged until we recognize the conflict for what it is and find some way to come to terms with our unreconstructed emotions.

While men are less susceptible to romanticism, they fall prey very easily to the new and insidious mythology— spawned by the sexual revolution and nurtured by rock-pop culture—which has elevated sexual desire to some kind of ultimate value. Many women also believe that sex leads to love (thus doing nothing more than reversing the old formula). This is the kind of love we are said to "make," and it may be that the active verb appeals more to the modern spirit as well as to the male self-image, since it implies a degree of skill and control quite lacking in the verb "to fall."

Myths, like roles, have a tendency to flip into their opposites. Once we thought sex was disgusting; now we think it's sublime. Of course, sex *can* be both . . . and a lot of other things besides. Fun, for instance, or a bore; release, reassurance, ego massage, power play, social credit card, an art form, a business—the list goes on and on. In any case, it seems that contemporary sexual mores are often as absurd and inhibiting to genuine eroticism as the old sexual mores they supplanted.

As familiar patterns disintegrate, the ensuing uncertainty only seems to reinforce the deep-seated human need for some kind of bonding. As a bulwark against loneliness and alienation, pair formation remains, for most people, the most viable kind of bond. Whether we opt for traditional marriage or more experimental kinds of coupling, the basic satisfactions remain the same—and so do the basic difficulties, including the perennial problems of jealousy, possessiveness, power and dependency, entrapment and boredom. Moreover, we are subject to certain habits of attraction, and tend to choose, and be chosen by, the same kinds of people, over and over—people who approximate some fantasy ideal that has no application to the reality of our lives.

Many of the principles and problems of pairing also apply to the nonsexual bonds of parents and children, of friends living together, and of the various familial associations, both voluntary and hereditary. For the purpose of bonding is not just emotional support but sharing the burdens of finances, housekeeping, and child care—dealing with other personalities, other values and priorities which may be unacceptable to us: thus, many "marital" problems are common to all people living together.

We tend to bring into any design for living expectations and evaluations that may have no bearing upon the situation at hand. For these and other reasons, living-together arrangements seem to work best when there are strong ties of affection, as well as some binding purpose beyond the purely practical one of sharing the load—a common faith, a work project, a mutual goal for the future.

The love of friendship may not be the most intense (there

is the distinct possibility that intensity, or excitement, might exist in some kind of inverse relation to depth of feeling), but it may well be love at its purest—pure in the sense of being free of ulterior motives. While friendship, too, is often bedeviled by competition and betrayal, it does tend to offer more psychological space and greater acceptance of realities than other types of love. Friendship is open-ended enough to accommodate divergences in tastes and opinions; it allows us to relate to different people on different levels, and to accept the fact that no one human being can, or should have to, fulfill all our needs.

I believe that the trust and tolerance and truthfulness that characterize friendship at its best can heal and save all intimate affiliations. Being a good friend—whether to yourself, your mother, your child, or the person sharing your bed—means first of all, respecting the integrity of the individual. We must allow our friends to be who they really are, instead of who we think they are, or wish them to be.

Common to all levels of love is the question of how to achieve trust and intimacy without commitment. And how define commitment? Forever, or for the duration—and if the latter, is it truly commitment? Freedom was defined by one young man as the ability to leave—to opt out. People who wish to escape the entrapment of pairing must find a balance between this kind of freedom and the minimal commitment necessary for any form of bonding, or loving, to succeed. For it is always easier, and seemingly safer, to run an old pattern into the ground than to experiment with a totally new one, and many people are quite willing to settle for what the novelist Djuna Barnes has called "the secure torment." They may think they want love, but security is the name of the game; these are the people who are apt to feel that any kind of "relationship" is better than none.

Love, in the cosmic, spiritual sense, means compassion, generosity—a feeling that comes from a fullness that spills over rather than an emptiness that needs to be filled. Such love is possible only where there is a degree of inner detachment—keeping a certain center of oneself inviolate. While one remains open, the inner core is not touched, and one can be hurt but not damaged. Thus one gains perspective on one's own feelings and those of others. We need not be saints to aspire to compassion. But it does help if we can learn to be a little less greedy, a little less frightened, a little less programed about what love *ought* to be.

There is no pretense, in this book, of scientific method or statistical verisimilitude. I do not believe that there is an objective truth in the realm of feelings. Nor do I offer any apologies for the fact that I am not an expert in anything. It seems to me that too many private areas are being pre-empted by the experts, and that too many people are altogether too willing, not to say anxious, to delegate responsibility for their lives to someone else.

Though I am not presumptuous enough to offer answers, I have tried to raise some questions. There are insights I would like to share, as well as some simple, home-tested recipes for dealing with emotional future shock, during this period of transitional misery. Unlike instruction manuals, recipes not only can but *should* be adjusted to individual tastes and means; they are merely suggestions, and there is no guarantee the results will satisfy everyone.

Above all, recipes are individual, rather than social and collective accomplishments—one person exploring and experimenting, perhaps comparing notes with other solitary searchers. In the beginning, I did not know exactly what I was looking for. Like a detective, I sniffed out clues. Though I found no culprits, only victims, I did discover connections; despite the confusions and contradictions, certain patterns seemed to emerge. Since my search involved, to a large extent, evaluating new mythologies and current doctrines, the women and men I talked with were mostly those who have tried, and are trying still, to live by the principles of equality, sexual emancipation, and alternatives to traditional marriage. For many of these people, including myself, such goals were generated by inner necessity rather than popular concern—long before they had names and labels.

Though the men and women I talked with ranged in age

from twenty to fifty, and in annual incomes from zero to six-digit figures, their lifework, like my own, might be considered marginal to society at large. Educated and unconventional to varying degrees, we are writers, editors, artists, actors, teachers, small entrepreneurs, Jacks-and-Jills of all trades—which no doubt places us somewhat outside the mainstream of America. Formed by a sophisticated urban environment (even if many of us now live in the suburbs or the country), we had access to the great liberation facilitators: enough leisure and enough money (ours or someone else's) and the proximity of a wide spectrum of information and experience.

A privileged lot, indeed, you might think. Yet it is precisely people like ourselves who are currently in the worst predicament . . . caught in between, stranded on the outer edges of the various movements, unable to go along completely with *any* program, having tried, and often failed, to put into practice some of the not-so-new ideas currently in vogue. One of my friends said, "Pioneers are always sad." Perhaps. But we do serve a function: we are able to set up a few guideposts for those who have lately jumped on the liberation band wagons, or are thinking of doing so. For while we represent no statistical cross section, what we have learned through trial and error may have a great deal of relevance for others, and the experiences herein recounted are by no means so special that they cannot be comprehended by most people.

Before I ever thought of this book, I began talking to people in an effort to learn whether I was all alone with my problems. To my great relief, I found that my life and times, which had seemed so unprecedented, turned out to have been not so extraordinary after all. Of course, the *details* are different, the personality unique, and from this point of view, every life is one-of-a-kind. But looking at correspondences rather than differences, I was struck again and again by how essentially similar we all are—women and men and children—how few are the variations on the basic human emotions.

romance

1
The Zap

All our recent cultural upheavals—the sexual revolution, women's liberation, the terminal illness of the institution of marriage—have not weakened the myth that falling in love will solve our emotional problems and provide instant fulfillment. Nor has the outward emancipation of women noticeably diminished female emotional slavery. On the contrary, the New Woman is more than ever desperate to fall in love and "have a relationship," as a lot of men who exploit this fact know, consciously or not. "I dig you, but I must be free," is the male cry. But the woman, though she may agree with the sentiment in principle, is stuck with her needs, her dreams and hopes, her ravenous hunger for love, sweet love, all you need is love, that's the one thing that there's just not enough of.

The propaganda hasn't stopped for a minute, and the pop songs still peddle the same old wares, the same self-deprecating attitudes, even if the language is hip and up-to-date. "When my soul was in the lost-and-found, you came along to claim it." *This* particular lyric could only have been written by a woman.* A man in love may go through changes too, but he's not likely to wait for a woman to claim his soul.

That psychosexual abnormality known as falling in love, with its heady mixture of ecstasy and misery, has always had and no doubt always will have its place in the human psyche. But it is *not* a basis for cohabitation . . . let alone a lifetime contract. Whatever needs and desires it answers for a time, falling in love tends to create problems rather than solve them. The most famous and violent fallings often occur with partners who are totally unsuitable from society's point of view (Romeo and Juliet, Tristan and Isolde) and/or unsuitable in terms of temperament and everyday living. History and legend abound with examples showing that falling in love can indeed be very dangerous—even fatal. From Greek myth to Italian opera to Tennessee Williams, the most moving love stories invariably have tragic endings.

It is a very recent notion, and a thoroughly American one, this idea that we have the right not only to hope but to *expect* that we will fall in love and marry the one we have fallen in love with. In former times, and in other cultures even today, falling in love may be the stuff for jokes, heartache, or tragedy, depending on the status of the parties involved, but it seldom impinges upon the normal business of marriage, family, and children.

Insecurity is practically built into the situation. By delivering yourself into the hands of just one person on whom your center of gravity depends, you have made yourself helplessly vulnerable; you have forfeited peace of mind and will be tossed between joy and sorrow at the loved one's whim. Wouldn't you say this state of affairs is a mixed blessing, at best? In fact, it's rather frightening. Yet this dependency is precisely what most women want.

Simone de Beauvoir has pointed out in *The Second Sex* that it is agonizing for a woman to assume responsibility for her own life. "Love for a woman is a mystic, a religious experience," she writes.

* "Natural Woman," Carole King.

She desires ... to amalgamate her inessential self
to some higher being—God or lover. She chooses to
desire her enslavement so ardently that it will
seem to her the expression of her liberty. ... The
annihilation of love is in fact an avid will to exist.
When a woman gives herself completely, she hopes
her idol will give her at once possession of herself
and of the universe he represents.

Most of the time, a woman does not succeed in deifying
any of the men she knows, De Beauvoir observes. Fortunately, one might add. Man is no more able to be the god
women seek than woman can be the goddess men long for
and fear.

More recently, Germaine Greer warned us, in *The Female Eunuch:*

Women must recognize in the cheap ideology of being in love the essential persuasion to take an irrational, self-destructive step. Such obsession has
nothing to do with love, for love is not swoon or
mania but a cognitive act, indeed the only way to
grasp the innermost core of personality.

One might envy Greer her assurance, if her personal life
did not suggest that she too might be finding it hard to
straddle the gap between what we know and what we are
able to do with that knowledge ... that she too, like the rest
of us, may have difficulty distinguishing between being in
love and loving.

In *Man's World, Woman's Place*, Elizabeth Janeway explains that, when a woman tries to lose herself in love, she
seems to be not so much giving up her own identity as asking for the lover's, and that is hard to grant. We have too
much riding on the emotion of love, and more is asked than
can be given.

When the response is felt to be inadequate, un-
satisfied greed is added to anxiety; highly unpleasant emotions to encounter where we have
been told to look for pleasure. Both can rise where
human relationships gather about themselves dis-
proportionate feelings of hope and obligation.

This feeling of connection as obligation haunts our era, according to Janeway. It seems to haunt, in particular, the male of our species. Men, too, dream of falling in love with the "right" woman. But their longing is tempered by a very strong fear and reluctance vis-à-vis love, despite the fact that they have less at stake.

That wise old man, James Stephens, long ago described the crucial difference between men and women in love:

> A man in love submits only to a woman, a partial, individual and temporary submission, but a woman who is loved surrenders to the very God of love himself, and so she becomes a slave and is not only deprived of her personal liberty but is even infected in her mental processes by this crafty obsession.

One might think women would shun this "crafty obsession" like the plague. Instead, we go courting emotional disaster with an alacrity that stuns the mind. Doris Lessing talks, not without bitterness, about "that yearning anguish we call being in love," in that chilling tale of contemporary marriage, "Not A Very Nice Story."

> The point was not the making love, but the spilling of emotion afterwards, the anguish, the guilt. Emotion was the point. Great emotion has been felt, had been suffered.... Everyone had got it wrong: the real motive for such affairs was the need to suffer the pain and yearning afterwards. ... We need the condition of being in love, of feeling "all that."

Ms. Lessing's analysis begs the question: What is so marvelous about being in love and feeling "all that"? Why is it worth so much turmoil, anxiety and grief?

One who tried to answer this question was Sophie, a twenty-two-year-old artist and model. Her looks and manner reflect the soft, fey, diffident style currently in vogue. But her words reflect a mind capable of cutting through the idealism of the youth culture. Sophie left home at the age of sixteen—she comes from a well-to-do Connecticut family torn by alcoholism and divorce. Since then she has traveled around the country, visiting communes, and already has several love affairs behind her.

"I used to believe I would find the key in another person," Sophie said. "Because I once had this psychedelic experience without drugs—with a man. But, of course, after I opened up with this man, six months later everything closed up again, to the point where I couldn't even feel anybody touching me. I sort of relived my mother's two marriages within half a year—this thing of I-had-to-suffer. I had to be a martyr and rise above it. And I picked the worst bastard in the world—well, maybe he wasn't such a bastard, but I was willing to be such a martyr that I stayed on no matter what he did.

"I was creating the whole thing for myself," she continued. "It was such absolute crap; it was my first love affair and it had to be a certain way. And I really didn't love him at all."

Sophie thought she knew better now. "You're your own key and you have to open yourself to yourself." Did that mean she had given up on romance? Not a chance. For the past year she had been living with a young man, eighteen years old, and here's what she had to say about that:

"When you're in love, you love yourself, and that's what makes everything beautiful. When I was first with Tommy, I never looked in mirrors. And when I did, I looked beautiful, whereas most of the time I look grotesque to myself."

By all objective standards, Sophie was lovely to look at. I asked what happened when the vibrations of daily life cracked the mirror, or shattered it altogether. She grew thoughtful. "You have to outlast the bad humps," she said, "and slowly work yourself back to the same point, on a more realistic level."

I suggested that love affairs might have a built-in time limit: that you were fortunate if you could develop in parallel ways. "You have to fight for that," said Sophie, with a look of determination in her gentle eyes that indicated she would stubbornly hang in, way past the deadline ... would play the martyr again, if necessary, in order to "work it out."

The belief that you are supposed to "work" on love, and even "fight" for it, seems to be a powerful one indeed for women, the kind of faith that can, at times, move mountains of male obstinacy and disinclination. The woman usually feels it's up to her to make the "relationship" succeed, and she will accept endless suffering, endless humiliation in the belief that it's the price one has to pay for love and whatever magical boon is to be gained from it. She is convinced that being in love is essential to her self-esteem, and that she is incomplete without it. And so she will put up with all kinds of abuse, ignore all the signs of deterioration, all the damage to her psyche (and her partner's) in order to keep the dream of love alive.

"It's the imagination that's involved," said a woman who has been having an affair with a married man for fourteen years. "I'm a tremendous builder. I have erected a mighty structure. And that, if you'll forgive me, is what love is about."

It is interesting to note that such an attitude implies, along with much self-control and self-denial, no small degree of arrogance. *She* is the builder, the one who controls the well-being of the affair. But think of the responsibility ... think of the *guilt* when that mighty structure crumbles, as it so often does, despite our best efforts!

A man, recently divorced, commented: "It must be an incredible accident when people stay in synch over long periods of time—when they get over bad parts and stagger along, and grow, or even dwindle, but in synch. The point is, when you get out of synch, there's nothing left—not even fight. Who are you, and what are you doing in my bed?"

The "imaginative" woman would reply that you have to "work" at staying in synch, though what exactly this work consists of is not very clear. It would seem to be largely a matter of compliance, devotion, perseverance, and certain romantic trappings which, from the evidence, symbolize far more to the woman than they do to the man.

Heather is one such exponent of the work ethic in love. She is thirty-two, lives in London with her seven-year-old daughter, and works hard at a career in broadcasting. She also works hard at her relations with men. Born in Ceylon and raised in provincial England, Heather married young, against the advice of family and friends. Though the marriage was, in her word, a "disaster" almost from the start, she stuck it out for over five years—the last two spent mostly "waiting," alone with her infant daughter. She then lived with another man for five years, and this affair has recently come to an end.

During those ten years, Heather was out of work less than a year, in order to have her baby, and often during her marriage she was the sole provider. "When we were both still at university, I would work at the post office during Christmas vacations, sorting mail and so on," she explained. "But no, he couldn't, because he had to do a lot of reading, which usually meant drinking in the pubs. Whenever we were in financial trouble, it was always me who went out and did jobs which were unpleasant. *He* couldn't compromise his integrity."

However, Heather admitted to being completely dependent emotionally on her men. "I think I am too much of a romantic and regard that as part of my weakness," she explained. "To me, a relationship is something that has to be closely looked after . . . guarded. Everything has to be right; literally, candles on the dinner table every night. I'd go to great lengths to prepare things nicely so that when Raymond [her recent lover] got back from work, which was always late, around nine, we would sit and eat together. Occasionally, it was a bit difficult when he would insist on taking his meal and going to sit in front of the telly."

I remarked that a man might just not feel like having dinner by candlelight *every* night. And in fact, Raymond left her for a girl who, according to Heather, was flighty and irresponsible. "I think he was a little overpowered by what I felt for him," she said ruefully. "He thought he did not love me as much as I loved him." Heather admitted that the man in her life took precedence, to a large extent, over her own child. Obviously, not all men find the burden of such devotion to their liking.

Having overinvested in romance, modern woman has become a beggar. She grovels for a crumb of love. No longer does she need a man so she may have food in her belly and a roof over her head, to protect her and her children, or secure her social position. When she *had* those needs and suffered in a bad marriage, at least she did not offer up her soul for a few soft words or an orgasm. She had her pride, the dignity of someone dealing with and making the best of a harsh reality.

But what are we to make of the sophisticated urban woman, winner of the sexual revolution, conquerer of the feminine mystique, the triumphant product of centuries of psychic labor? What means that look of hunger and desperation in her eyes? Why does she fidget so nervously with her false eyelashes? She has another date with the assistant buyer in her office, who earns three thousand dollars a year less than she does, and maybe tonight he'll be able to get it up. She knows she must be patient and relaxed, but she is anxious and the Martinis haven't taken the edge off the jitters. Her analyst has explained it all—it's *his* problem, nothing to do with her. But why, oh why, does it happen so often? What is it she does wrong, or fails to do right? She checks the mirror, but it tells her nothing. She knows she looks good, as good as she can look, and better than most. She knows how to make a man feel comfortable, how to talk and entertain when called for and be quiet at other times, how to let him know she likes sex without being aggressive. Her apartment is charming—her books, her records, her cuisine . . . everything is beyond reproach. She appears intact, but the pain of lovelessness has hollowed her out; loneliness has emptied her till there is nothing but this enormous aching void inside, growing bigger every day, pushing against the glossy outer shell.

She reads the latest magazines and all the latest books on sex; of course she is "good in bed." It is the *sine qua non* of the competition for the ever-more-elusive male. But she does not really enjoy sex . . . she cannot enjoy sex while she is consumed with anxiety and sorrow over the coldness and inhumanity of her sexual encounters.

Joan Didion, in *Slouching Towards Bethlehem*, tells us how she

> had watched them in supermarkets and she knew the signs. At seven o'clock on a Saturday evening they would be standing in the checkout line reading the horoscope in *Harper's Bazaar* and in their carts would be a single lamb chop and maybe two cans of cat food and the Sunday morning paper, the early edition, with the comics wrapped outside. They would be pretty some of the time, their skirts the right length, their sunglasses the right tint, and maybe only a little vulnerable tightness around the mouth, but there they were, one lamb chop, some cat food and the morning paper.

To forestall the fate of one lamb chop, we are often forced to make do. Rachel, one victim of the liberation void, outwardly appears the quintessential New York career girl. She arrived from Oklahoma five years ago and has "made it," at the age of twenty-eight, in the toughest business in the toughest city in the world. All her childhood dreams have come true, she told me. She wanted to be a fashion buyer on Fifth Avenue, and she is. She wanted to go to Europe, and she goes at least twice a year. A glamorous life indeed, yet Rachel has spent many evenings alone, wearing the same old jeans and sweater, her elegant wardrobe neglected in closets—depressed, confused, wondering what was missing. Or else she was frantically running around—to her shrink, her yoga class, her consciousness-raising—getting worn out, as she wondered what was *still* missing even with all her spare time accounted for. What was missing, of course, was the Dream of Dreams: Love and Marriage. At the time of our talk she was "living" with a young man who did not suit her at all; she admitted she had not—"even for thirty seconds"—considered Carl a marital possibility. Nevertheless, she asked him to move in with her the first night they got together. "At the time I met Carl I had a tremendous need for somebody . . . anybody . . . around me. I'd gone out with a lot of men and not found anybody I was attracted to, for a very long time. Then one freaky night this guy comes over and I was just so ready for it . . . someone I could dig, mentally and physically."

I asked why she had to have him living with her. I knew her well enough to point out that Carl spent more nights away from her apartment than in it; that she was always waiting for him to call and let her know if he was coming "home" or not.

"I've thought about it a lot and not reached any positive conclusions," said Rachel. "I know a lot of bullshit goes down. Yet I'm putting up with it and not really hating it."

What *was* she getting out of it, I wondered, since all she did was complain about his sloppy habits (Rachel is compulsively neat) and his spending most of their evenings together on the telephone.

"I think maybe Carl is a study to me," said Rachel. "Someone I cannot figure out. Someone who not only says he doesn't want a relationship, but really doesn't. I didn't believe him for a while, or thought enough of my ability to make him come 'round, but I must say for him that he told me where it was at right from the start."

Ah, yes! I dig you, but I must be free. But Carl was not honest enough to say, "No, I'm not going to move my cats and my stuff into your place." He's not above exploiting Rachel's hopes and illusions. No ties, but why not take advantage of the home comforts she has to offer?

And from Carl's point of view, why not indeed? It is, to a

large extent, a question of supply and demand. When there
are so many more women than men who are ravenous for
romance ... when smart, sensible women sleep with a guy
once or twice and say, "Move in with me"—well, then,
something has to give. There are a lot of men who make it
a practice to live the way Carl does. It's not cold-blooded—
they *like* the woman. She's got a nice place. So they move
into the ready-made nest and play house for a while ...
until they get bored or restless or find someone they like
better. They have not helped to build the nest, they are not
really involved or committed. Sometimes they contribute to
household expenses. Quite often they don't. The woman
figures she has to pay the rent anyway.

Since this type of arrangement was designed to fill the
vacuum that nature is said to abhor, it could well prove
satisfactory to both parties, if only they could accept it for
what it is. There are no more rules, after all. But the
women are mostly anxious, insecure, and resentful. This is
not what they want. (The answer to Freud's classic question, What do women really want? is: *Everything!* All the
comforts and securities of the old plus all the rights and
privileges of the new.)

And the men are largely foot-loose and alienated and un-
satisfied. Somehow, this isn't what they want either. For
manhood, as defined in our society, involves not only power
but responsibility, obligation, honor. Men of liberationist
persuasion, eager to escape the provider trap, are relinquish-
ing responsibility along with power, unaware that they are
thereby cutting themselves off from their identity as men.
For, as yet, no substitute definitions are available to them.

And for women, identity is still tied up with caring for a
man ... or a child. This fact may account, in part, for the
trend to have babies without husbands. Having given birth,
your womanhood is proved once and for all. And when
you're in love, or living with a man, your womanhood is also
safe, for a time—even if you're miserable. Both Rachel and
Heather admitted that the appeal of the man "with one foot
out the door" is not just the challenge he represents. He also

allows the woman more control over her life. If—or rather, *when*—he leaves, it will hurt, but it will not destroy the fabric of her existence.

The dilemma of modern woman has not gone unnoticed or unremarked on by the psychoanalytic establishment. "Certain free-living women are apt to have trouble finding and holding on to satisfactory males," according to Doctors Ferdinand Lundberg and Marynia Farnham, authors of *Modern Woman, The Lost Sex*. Though their language and bias are grimly Freudian and there is the implication that it is women who are to blame, the doctors nevertheless give a fairly accurate description of some men's fear of women. Men, they write,

> usually sense some lack of true tenderness [read: subservience] about them . . . they come to feel . . . that they are confronted with an adversary, a rival. . . . Unable to hold the fully masculine man, such a woman perforce falls back on the passive-feminine, juvenile and even homosexual male.

Now the "passive-feminine" man is apt to be a very good lover—a far better lover, in fact, than the "fully masculine" man. His anima is strong—that is, the female aspect of his own nature is well-developed, and thus he "understands" women. He may appreciate women too, but in any case he knows exactly how to get around them. Such a man is often the Don Juan type—unable or unwilling to enter into associations of true mutuality and commitment, he will step with impunity where other men fear to tread. Don Juan is only playing at the game of love, and he is confident of victory. He's not afraid of the Big Bad Bitch. In any event, he is sexually potent, and he can be had. The New Woman may know what he is—deep down, as they say—but beggars can't be choosers. What's more, beggars seem to have an almost limitless capacity to deceive themselves.

Even if the woman understands the exigencies of the times and accepts the man as he is, often the man cannot

accept himself. He's got an image problem; he feels humili-
ated and deeply resents his dependent position. If power
corrupts, weakness corrupts even more; dependency under-
mines character in a subtle and insidious way. The man
tends to become spoiled, vain, deceitful, selfish (all the things
women have been accused of in the past). He is accustomed
to thinking in hierarchical terms, and his attitude is: "O.K.,
if I can't be in charge, *you* take care of things." But this
reversal of roles brings no more rewards than the old pattern did. It is easier to do the opposite of what was done
before than to try something totally new. The woman, of
course, needs someone she can, if not lean on, at least rely
on once in a while—no goddess she. But she finds she is
saddled with a pampered child, or a man whose behavior, if
not downright sadistic, can best be described as "bitchy."
She herself has spoiled him, and he knows he can do whatever he likes.

What this type of man likes to do, much of the time, is
get high. For a long time I wondered why so many attractive, capable women fall in love with drunkards and junkies,
the kind of men who are on something or other every moment of their waking day. Here's one clue: it feeds the
female dream of the Beautiful Prince. If only the spell
could be broken (by love of course—what else?) . . . if only he
could cast off his ugly-toad disguise (always the doing of
some impersonal evil force like booze or dope) and emerge
the Beautiful Prince we just *know* dwells beneath, then we
will love each other and live happily ever after. For if a
man has his life together and turns out not to be a Beautiful
Prince but a chauvinist pig, then the dream goes by the
boards. And so we find it easier to love the losers, the also-
rans, the ones with permanently jammed "potential." There
are a lot of them around, for one thing. And if they are
chronically drugged, dropped-out, and unemployed . . . if
they are childish and more than a little gay, so much the
worse for us. At least our servitude is freely given, not demanded by an autocratic superior. If the unconscious element of contempt for the man's weakness makes us feel

guilty, this causes us to dote on him even more. And the man, who loves his drugs more than he loves his woman, usually knows what's happening. His resentment is, in a way, justified. For the woman's motives in taking up with him are highly suspect. She may want to nurse him or reform him. In any case, the man knows she's not dealing with the reality of him as he is, even if she often agrees to get high with him against her own inclinations.

What happens typically in such a ménage is that the woman goes out to work, often at some slave labor like office work or waitressing, while the man stays home and indulges in fantasies of writing, painting, playing music, or whatever else he pretends to be into aside from his *real* occupation, which is getting stoned. It is assumed that (a) menial jobs are easier to get for women, who can disguise their own unconventionality more easily, and this is largely true; (b) such work is less devastating to the woman's psyche, since her "balls" (meaning pride, ego, integrity) are not at stake; and (c) a man's artistic efforts, however inept, are always to be taken seriously, whereas a woman's creative endeavors, even when of obvious excellence, are always secondary to the more basic requirements—that she be attractive, compliant, good-natured, and, above all, uncritical. She must not be a "bring-down," must never show what Joyce Carol Oates describes as "that touch of common-sense irony that loses us all our men."

Here's the scene: Joan has worked hard all day in her office. She gets home around six and starts to prepare dinner for several guests, including myself. She discovers she needs a couple of things from the store. Ben, her lover-in-residence who is out of a job and whom she supports, says halfheartedly, "I'll go get them." But Joan detects the truculence in his voice and says hastily, "No, it's O.K. I'll just run out and do it." She comes back and cooks the dinner, while Ben drinks and chats with the guests. After we eat, she clears the table, washes the dishes, and finally sits down to relax. I ask her, at an opportune moment, why she didn't let Ben go to the store or help with the dishes, which he also, in the same tentative way, offered to do. "Oh," she says, "he's really a terrible shopper, always gets the wrong brand and overpays. And I'm used to my kitchen, really don't like anyone else cluttering around in there." She adds, with a self-deprecating smile, "You know how compulsive I am."

Joan is afraid that if she doesn't please Ben and cater to him, he will leave her for another woman. There are a number of her friends who wouldn't hesitate to snap him up and install him in their own apartments, for Ben is attractive and charming. What's more, that subsex, man-as-lover, is an endangered species. Joan knows this in her nerves and viscera, if not with her mind.

Out in the communes and communities of the counter-culture, the women have also assumed a deliberately marginal and supportive role. "Breadbakers," a young woman in Woodstock called them, contemptuously. It's all very fine, bread as sacrament and holy macrobiotic food, but it is the women who cook and bake the bread even when the men don't work the land, and mostly they don't. The women don't play music, they *listen*. What's more, the necessary cash usually comes from parents who are more loath to let daughters fend for themselves than sons. For many young women, this money is like a marriage portion—a bribe to be accepted into a scene.

Of course, women have always worked to support their men's artistic and intellectual efforts. I am not just referring to the wife who works to see her husband through law or medical school, with the hope of eventually gaining a prosperous and status-filled life. My own maternal grandmother gave birth to nine children (of whom six lived) and ran a tobacco shop all her life in order to support the family while grandfather spent his days studying the Torah —not even in the practical capacity of rabbi but purely as an intellectual and spiritual exercise. Her circumstance was not unusual and had the full support and approval of the ghetto communities of Poland and Russia. And women throughout the ages, finding themselves married to drunkards, have accepted their "widowhood" and gone to work.

It does seem odd, however, that there are so many of these arrangements at a time when women are ostensibly emerging from oppression. Also, the men are often not doing anything at all—they are dropouts from the intellectual, spiritual, and artistic life as well as the conventional world. Yet they seem to have no trouble finding women who will support them, emotionally as well as financially.

Oh, the women don't *like* it. They complain, they fret. But they put up with it. Whatever the price, they must have it—that special thrill, that quickening in the gut. That sweet surrender. Love is the answer . . . even though we've forgotten the question. If there ever really *was* a question.

I talked about love and dependency and compromise with my friend Lanie. At thirty-nine, with two divorces behind her, a boy of fourteen and a girl of seven to look after, and with her health and spirits seriously undermined by two operations, Lanie is still stunning; witty, full of vitality, she draws people to her, and while she has always been, as she puts it, "enormously successful" with men, at the same time she has always had close and enduring friendships with women. Both her husbands were a little intimidated by her—there was something wild and unpredictable about Lanie—yet she was a compulsive housekeeper and would slide into the domestic trap with self-destructive relish. Nevertheless, Lanie also worked as a schoolteacher, has written poetry, and recently published a novel. At the time we talked, she was having an affair with a young musician, ten years her junior, and debating whether or not she should allow him to move in with her.

"I've been thinking about Chuck," she said. "You know, he's really penniless. Now, at the moment, it is of no importance to me that I feed him and pay for movies and dinners out. . . ." However, Lanie admitted, it might well become important later on, especially if they lived together, for she is by no means rich.

In the beginning, everything is fine and the tendency is to let things ride—why not, since there are no more rules? But as soon as the bloom is off the romance, or the man fails us in some way, the hidden resentment will out. He didn't come home when he was supposed to and suddenly we are in a rage. He is taking unfair advantage ... we are being ripped off!

What he's taking advantage of is our yen for what Lanie calls the Zap. "We go for the plumage," she explained. "Man spreads his feathers and woman gets hung up on them, discovering later that that's all there is ... no substance. But I think you have to have it. It's the starting point, and without it you have nothing at all. You can be best of friends, but if there isn't that thing that says, Zap! Look at that! I've got to have that! That's *good!* then you have no basis for a relationship.

"True, the mating game has to be replaced with growth of some sort," Lanie agreed, "otherwise it dies. But the plumage—that's the energy force. The person has to be feeding you something. Look how beautiful the mind is ... it can be an infinite storehouse. A lifetime isn't enough, if you've got the right person."

Here we come to the heart of the matter. The truth is, we do not all that often fall in love with the "right" person. The Zap may well be triggered by someone who approximates some unconscious ideal—a parent, perhaps, or a movie star—someone who perpetuates a fantasy that we, as rational adults, might want no part of. On one sexual-emotional level, we are drawn to opposites, to people who, as Anais Nin puts it in *The Diary of 1931–1934,* "act out for us a self we cannot and do not wish to act out." On another level of love, as in friendship, we seek out people similar to ourselves. Here, the romantic fanfare may be missing, the weak knees and palpitating heart ... it may be someone we're not in the habit of being attracted by, not our "type," too much like ourselves to produce the tension, the electricity we associate with being in love.

"I think I am more centered on attraction than on love,"

Lanie confessed. Many people fail to distinguish between the two, or else assume one will automatically follow the other. The Zap is very popular, in our speedy times; one hesitates to introduce the quaint, old-fashioned notion of a soul mate. Modern woman would scorn to admit that's what she's missing, as she leaps from affair to affair, getting no real satisfaction—she's not sure there *is* such a thing as a soul mate.

What's more, the sexual-emotional Zap is powerful. It cannot and should not be dismissed. Lanie believed this instinctive drawing to someone is positive. "Though people are destructive, there is also the instinct for survival, and people are turned on to someone who is right for them," she said. "But they destroy whatever it is they want in that person. Their conditioning fucks them up. You cannot help being attracted, and you cannot keep yourself from destroying."

Lanie and I have known each other for years; we share a tendency to be attracted to men of dark, demonic natures —men who possess a certain kind of Dionysian energy that charges us. It may be that these men do something important for our psyches. They represent unassimilated aspects of our own natures, a yearning for chaos and irresponsibility, for living on the edge, where there is danger but the perceptions are more real. How our conditioning fucks us up is that we immediately seek to get ourselves into a domestic arrangement with these men. We have a basic need for order and stability, and so we try to make these men truthful, honorable, reliable—everything they are not. Part of woman's penchant for "working" on love is this desire to have it both ways. If the men refuse to be what we want them to be, we grow indignant and distraught— how can they be such bastards, why don't they appreciate what we're trying to do for them? But it is obvious that if we are going to be drawn to such men, for perhaps sound psychological reasons, we have to forget about living with them and domesticating them, about expecting anything other than the connection of the moment.

"I thought of tying in with Chuck because he has this energy," mused Lanie. "But then maybe I shouldn't be with him at this stage of my life, when I need mellowing, not more excitement."

Even if it were possible to give up on the excitement of the Zap, it would not seem worthwhile to many people. Like Lanie, they will continue to act out the cycle: attraction, approach-avoidance, power struggle, rejection, disappointment, pain. At least Lanie is likely to maintain some degree of detachment, even self-mockery, throughout these gyrations.

Recognizing the pattern helps a lot. When a lover you discover at your gates, my friend, *do* take a second look. You may find he's remarkably like your exes. The "blindness" of love is largely self-imposed. If you can keep your eyes open and still want to take a chance on romance, then do so with an awareness of the risks involved, and if things don't work out, don't rail against your fate, the treachery of men, or even your analyst, who has still not cured you of your neuroses.

Most people have no very clear idea of what they are looking for in a mate. They wait for the magical Zap, and when it happens, that's it! That's the given, the raw material we have to "work" with. Love conquers all! But even if we do know what we want and need, we must face the fact that we may not be able to get it. There is, for the New Woman, an indisputable shortage of comparable men. We have to ask ourselves if we are willing and able to compromise, accept provisional situations, consent to share love with men who are not our ideals. And if we cannot, we must be prepared to do without.

There is a certain type of man with whom the New Woman can find romance, provided she is able to make the necessary psychic adjustments. One of the little ironies to come out of women's liberation is a strong, if largely unacknowledged, fascination with the totally unreconstructed, animalistic, supermasculine male. Burt Reynolds in center-

OKANAGAN REGIONAL LIBRARY

fold glory! Call it nostalgia. These men have the appeal of the exotic, the forbidden . . . the endangered wild species.

Germaine Greer set the pace, with her union-card–carrying ironworker. But such couples are to be found everywhere . . . the major writer and the shaggy woodsman; the editor and the truck driver; the decorator and the waiter. What's happening in these liaisons is a breakdown of the barriers of class—and often, of the barriers of age as well. When educated, liberated, middle-class women consort with men of lower socioeconomic levels or of different age groups, they are breaking all sorts of unwritten rules. We internalize society's values more than we like to admit, and there is still a vast difference in the way the world, and consequently the woman herself, views this business of mating. A man of distinction and talent may marry his housekeeper, and no one will think the less of him. But a woman is supposed to mate upward—the man should be as high as she is on the social ladder, if not higher—and her status *still* depends to a large extent on her husband, no matter what she has going on her own.

Of course, this social dictum has been flaunted before—D. H. Lawrence's Lady Chatterley and Ibsen's Miss Julie were doing it long before the advent of Greer *et al.* In our time, the proletarian stud can seem a welcome relief indeed after all those New Impotence professional men, all those drugged-out parasites. He has a very clear idea of what it means to be a man. He doesn't talk about his shrink, or blame his mother, or worry about being gay.

Above all, he has the proper attitude toward the woman's career. He may be impressed, he may even be proud that she's so smart, but he's not competing and therefore not threatened. How can he be in awe of her when he fucks her every night and she moans and begs for more? (The mere fact that he fucks her already makes her a little contemptible in his view.) He has his own life, his innocent *macho* assurance. There is a distance between him and the woman —it may be a healthy, necessary distance. They do not share everything. They do not mess with each other's minds.

The back-to-basics appeal of this type of man may also lie in a certain *kind* of sexuality—what the noted sociologist Jessie Bernard calls the body-centered kind, which has been largely discredited by civilized society in favor of the person-centered kind. But there remains in many women a longing for this earlier, more primitive sexual mode. Bernard points out, in her study of contemporary mating mores, *The Sex Game*, that even those women most insistent on equality of the sexes may recoil at being deprived of their sexuality: "It can be as frustrating not to have one's sexuality recognized and appreciated as it is to have it the only thing recognized and appreciated."

"Only the bad guys are sexy," one woman told me years ago. At the time she was heavily involved with a series of black *machos*, all of whom practiced pimp psychology, based on the premise that the worse you treat a woman the better she likes it. The "bad guys"—Casanovas, *machos*, gigolos— may get angry at women, may even abuse them, but they are not intimidated to the point of impairing their physical or emotional virility.

Renata felt she could take on a lover from a different social milieu without undue strain. A widely traveled cosmopolite in her forties, she has lived and loved in London, Paris, New York, and California. Renata was married and divorced years ago and has lived with a number of men since. The public Renata is clever, attractive, articulate, and knows her way around. The private Renata, whom she described as "neurotic but sober," revealed herself in a note of urgency, of controlled desperation, beneath the cool, mocking inflection of her voice.

"While our need is to be with someone whose interests are similar to our own, someone we can have a dialogue with, *their* need is not to be with us, and they invariably choose another kind of woman," she observed. "I've been aware of this for a long time, and I must tell you that I no longer need to be with a peer if there are other qualities that interest me ... like a certain approach to nature, to dealing with existence. These are powerful attributes, and a fisherman could have them—or someone who works for the electric company. But in our supposedly classless society we tend to get involved with chic and life styles, so that we are not really leading inventive or imaginative lives."

Renata meant that it was difficult for a woman like her to *meet* a fisherman or someone who works for the electric company. But she was quite prepared to go off to some remote part of the world where she thought there might be possibilities of lovers, if not mates. I expressed some doubt that she would really drop her life, her career, and her friends to go live in some fishing village in New Zealand.

"Oh, I'm due for some heavy traveling," said Renata. "My brain tells me I shouldn't, out of some loyalty to some abstraction, but my cunt says do it!"

What about her heart, I wanted to know, predicting she'd be climbing the walls within six months. "Fine," she said. "I'll come back then. You'll see me around. I'll give you a call."

We went on to talk about why women seem to need a peer and men do not—their women do not have to be "suitable" if they provide warmth and comfort, food and sex. "A man will rarely leave a woman because there's no longer any reason to be with her," said Renata. "He will only leave for someone to replace her. Men who are *into* relationships with women will not live alone for a moment, whereas a woman will live alone rather than with someone she's not attuned to. Women are braver, they are purer emotionally, more striving in what they want."

Like all generalizations, this one is open to question. Women are more available to men than the other way around, as has already been noted. If men are able to do without a peer mate, it may also be that they feel more complete in themselves. It may be that, unlike women, they have accepted a certain feeling of loneliness and alienation as part of the human condition. For despite the fact that women are so pure and striving emotionally, they are selling out like crazy, and it is definitely a buyer's market.

I asked Renata how she would feel if she had to spend

the rest of her life without a mate. "I've been confronted
with that possibility," she replied, "and I'd do *anything* to
avert it. I don't want to live alone. I've thought of making
it with another woman. But there's a continuity, a vertical-
ity that happens with the other sex . . . the woman thing is
inward, a form of narcissism, and some women prefer that.
But I'm attracted to men—it's an enormous force in my
life."

Although in theory there is no reason why the fisherman
or the construction worker should not prove a satisfactory
companion, in practice, however, the woman in such an
affair cannot resist tampering with the natural man—
teaching him how to dress, how to order in restaurants.
For if he is accepted as a lover and brought out of the
closet, then she is responsible for him in the eyes of the
world. She may know his true worth, the simple, honest
goodness of him, but what will her friends say? But once
the woman has succeeded in refining him, he may lose his
appeal for her—and, what is worse, she may lose all her
appeal for him.

It is not so easy for a woman to give up her dream of a
true mate, an equal and a partner—a man she can whole-
heartedly cherish and admire. The lover she accepts may
give her what she needs for a while—sex and affection and
loyalty—her batteries may be recharged, but she is not
satisfied. Something is missing; something is wrong. Always, it is the compromise, the second-best, which humili-
ates and breaks the heart.

2
The Cichlid Effect

To understand how the New Woman got herself into such a fix, we must look at what has happened on the liberation scene in the past fifteen or twenty years. At first, the goals of greater social freedom and a less restricted sex life seemed one and the same; as women aspired toward sexual emancipation, men were almost universally enthusiastic. It was part of the new culture trend, but more than that it was the age-old male fantasy come true. At last there would be women around who had sex because they enjoyed it, not because they wanted to bargain with it.

During the fifties and early sixties, the free-living and free-loving woman was a rarity. She was a rebel and a freak. With no power, no one to back her up, only her own *chutzpa*, she could be as outwardly arrogant and feisty as she liked. Nor were the quality or extent of her sexual emergence likely to imperil male supremacy. On the contrary, her behavior tended to reinforce the general belief in the erotic ascendancy of man. Women seeking a more rewarding sex life represented a fascinating challenge, especially if (as was usually the case) they were young and pretty. Thus they never lacked for men as sex partners, lovers, or friends. This was back in the days before Masters and Johnson revived, albeit inadvertently, the specter of the voracious and insatiably lustful female.

Things have changed dramatically in the past decade or so, and what was the exception is fast becoming the rule. After a sufficient number of men have been exposed long enough and often enough to a sufficient number of women who refuse to be subservient, in or out of bed, the challenge turns to threat, and there occurs the phenomenon that Jessie Bernard in *The Sex Game* has termed the "cichlid effect."

Konrad Lorenz studied a species of fish called cichlids, and had some difficulty determining which cichlids were male or female, since they not only looked alike but were also identical in their behavior patterns, including those of the sex act. How, he wondered, did the cichlids themselves know which of them was male and female. In time, Lorenz came up with the following discovery, which he describes in *On Aggression*:

> If the male has even the slightest fear of his partner, his sexuality is completely distinguished. In the female, there is the same relation between aggression and sexuality; if she is so little in awe of her partner that her aggression is not entirely suppressed, she does not react to him sexually at all ... [thus] a male can only pair with an awe-inspired and therefore submissive female, and a female only with an awe-inspiring and therefore dominant male.

People are not fish, of course, but zoological analogies can have instructive value. In the animal kingdom we can observe matriarchies, patriarchies, group marriages, till-death-us-do-part monogamy, tribal polygyny and polyandry, and total segregation of the sexes except for seasonal and ritual matings. There is even a species of fish wherein the leading female changes sex upon the death of the male;

she develops testicles and proceeds to become the ruler of the harem.

Musing upon the mating habits of the cichlids, one may well speculate that the male could really be terrified of the female, and perhaps of the very act of sex itself. The only way he can perform his essential function is to have the female assuage his fears by gestures of submission, and it is possible she must pretend to be more in awe of him than she actually is. (Apparently, cichlids of both sexes are naturally very aggressive.)

Among humans, there is supposedly no such thing as a true biological instinct. What we have in its place is myth. It is mythic compulsion that causes us to behave in an instinctive, reflexive manner that often goes counter to the dictates of reason. According to Joseph Campbell, in his study of mythology, *The Masks of God*, the myth of female weakness is an attempt to mask its opposite, the myth of female power, which "goes deeper, was born earlier, and is universal." He explains that in the earliest ages of human history, the magical force and wonder of the female and her reproductive powers were no less a marvel than the universe itself. And for millennia, it has been the chief concern of the male part of the population "to break, control and employ this prodigious power to its own ends."

But once sex is detached from pregnancy and women are free to bed whomever they choose, the myth of female weakness and vulnerability, so long and carefully nurtured, is seriously undermined. This destroys the delicate balance between the two myths, which coexist in the unconscious and are merely two sides of the same coin. Without the myth of female weakness, there remains only the terror of the all-powerful female, mother and goddess, witch and ogress, which has haunted the male psyche since infancy and the collective unconscious of the human race for as long as memory serves.

In *The Prisoner of Sex*, Norman Mailer, defending Henry Miller against the onslaughts of Kate Millet, described this primordial fear:

> [It] was man's sense of awe before woman, his
> dread of her position one step closer to eternity
> (for in that step were her powers) which made
> men detest women, revile them, humiliate them
> ...do everything to reduce them so that one
> might dare to enter them and take pleasure in
> them...for she is in their eyes already armed
> with the power that she brought them forth...
> the earliest etchings of memory go back to that
> woman between whose legs they were conceived,
> nurtured, and near-strangled in the hours of
> birth.

Even Mailer might admit that this gynephobia is not
necessarily an admirable trait. Moreover, it is the purpose
of cultural revolutions and the drive toward personal liberation to break the strangle hold such myths have over our
psyches. If we have not succeeded in this as well as we
might, the reason may well be that we have failed to understand the true nature of the problem. For disproving facts
is not at all the same as changing emotions, and to confuse
the two is in its own way a bit of mythic thinking. It is
the fallacy that Freud called "omnipotence of thought"—
the notion that the mind and the will control the world.

This form of mythic thinking is the peculiar weakness
of revolutionaries and progressives. For instance, the
liberation-minded man of good will and intentions is faced
with this horned dilemma: the spirit is willing—of course
he believes in freedom and equality for women—but the
flesh, tied to deep-seated desires, will have none of it. In his
secret heart he longs for the nurturing, compassionate
woman who fulfills all his needs and makes no demands. The
force of this longing comes from the dreams and memories
of infancy, when nothing was asked of us and all that we
wanted was given. Since we all had mothers, this subterranean longing is not peculiar to men. Women too long
for the paradise lost.

"What does a woman see in another woman that she does
not see in a man?" asked the poet Sylvia Plath. And she

answered herself: "Tenderness." This is the great lure of lesbianism; women, it is claimed, can find love only with other women because women are (read: *should* be) more gentle, understanding, compassionate. The fact is that women have always found it extremely difficult to live up to these mythic imperatives, even under the most powerful pressures and strictures.

The new ideal woman of the cultural revolution, with her long hair and old-fashioned dresses, baby at her breast—silent, intuitive, sexually generous, and undemanding—who is she but a reincarnation of the mother-goddess? You've come a long way, baby—full circle. Now let us look at the other new ideal woman of our times; she too has been around forever. She is the woman who broke the mold, the exceptional woman who was admired, respected, and—yes, it's *She*—venerated. She took on another role that could be understood. Joan of Arc was a general and a saint; Elizabeth I and Catherine I were rulers; Florence Nightingale was a healer, and so was Marie Curie (who, moreover, worked side by side with her husband). They were something more and other than women—they were mothers and goddesses.

Some of the leaders of the women's movement have marched straight into the trap. They are not seen as human beings striving for a more rewarding life but as embodiments of the dark, mythic figures of female power—devouring men like the evil goddess Kali. The spokeswomen for female liberation most often mentioned in tones of awe and (albeit grudging) admiration by the men I talked with were Valerie Solanas and Jill Johnston. When I pointed out that Valerie Solanas, author of the extremist *Scum Manifesto*, is not considered by anyone a *leader* of the woman's movement and, moreover, has been attested criminally insane, and that Jill Johnston, a dedicated lesbian holding to the extreme position of total separation of the sexes, did not speak for any women *I* knew, the men replied that they admired their "purity"... their "fervor." Ms. Johnston reminded one man of Joan of Arc. (On the other hand, they

had very little to say about Kate Millet or Gloria Steinem,
except to mention that Ms. Steinem is very good-looking.)

As a matter of fact, not all men are repelled by the myth
of female power. If there is fear, there is also fascination. I
know men who pride themselves, and rightly so, on never
having been male chauvinists. Somehow they have always
known the true worth of women. These men usually prefer
female company and some have only women friends (this
group includes a good number of male homosexuals). They
feel vindicated by recent events; there's an I-told-you-so
satisfaction in the way they feel about the women's liberation movement.

On the one hand, these men may have learned, perhaps
from observing their parents, that power must be paid for,
and the price may well be pleasure, intimacy, and support.
On the other hand, they tend to idolize and glorify women.
There is something suspect about such devotion—as if they
had decided that, since it was impossible to lick them, they
had best join them. These "women-lovers" too are in the
grip of the myth of female power. For, as Anais Nin observed in one of her early *Diaries*, "If a person continues to
see only giants, it means he is still looking at the world
through the eyes of a child."

Such men are often better feminists than women. As a
rule, they are counterculture men (automatically devalued
by society) and have little to lose, emotionally or socially,
by their liberationist stance. My friend Buddy has been a
champion of women for years. At forty-seven, he has been
twice married and divorced; he worked for many years as a
theatrical press agent. Buddy is very sympathetic to the
youth culture, feels out of touch with his own generation,
and likes to surround himself with young people. Six years
ago, before I ever thought of this book, Buddy told me,
"Women's liberation is the most important and exciting
thing happening today."

Nevertheless, Buddy considers himself a romantic. "I
still believe in the mystery of woman," he explained, "even

though I am friends with women and talk with them freely."

I suggested that a belief in mystery can actually be a stubborn refusal to understand. Women might be *complicated*, but so are men. I asked him what, in particular, he found so mysterious about us.

"Women's social behavior has a high radiance of optimism about it," said Buddy. "I love it. And it's mysterious. Men are not as optimistic. It's not masculine. A man is supposed to be ready to die. The male trip is that he's expendable—you send him out to wars to get killed.

"The drama is, the guy has an optimistic wife, and he's deep-down cynical and pessimistic. And what goes on between them is insane. You know that song . . . where he meets a beggar on a crutch who says, Why ask for so much? and a pretty woman in the door says, Why not ask for more?"

What Buddy said was true, in a way. I come from a family of martyred women—forever suffering, always *kvetching*, but with such *zest* . . . basically much more hopeful and ambitious than the men who were always saying, "Don't worry so much, it's going to be all right," not believing it for a moment.

I asked Buddy what it was he wanted from a woman. "An extension of my work potential," he replied, "so I can produce more things I would like to produce." In other words, for inspiration, said I. "Yes," he said, "a supportive situation for creativity." He too dreamed of the nurturing woman who would inspire and perhaps goad him on to glory. What he needed was her belief in him . . . her optimism.

A young Frenchman I talked with said that the women in Brittany, where he comes from, control everything. The men are away fishing, most of the time, and the women take care of the business of the town. Children inherit property from their mothers. My own background abounded with tough women. Most of the people I knew as a child had marriages similar to that of my mother and father. The women were dynamos and good-looking to boot; they were in business with their husbands and ran the show. The wives tended to be domineering and loudmouthed, while the husbands were soft-spoken and endlessly accommodating. An entire subculture operated that way, and if it produced monsters like Portnoy *mère*, what about the complicity, overt and covert, of Portnoy *père* and *fils*?

Marriages wherein the partners work out some kind of symbiosis are legion. For people have always been aware that, along with the myths, come certain facts—namely, that some men are superior to some women, and some women are superior to some men. If an aggressive woman found a man she could dominate, she did so—back in the days of innocence, before Freud and his concept of the castrating female began to plague women with guilt, forcing them to turn their aggressions inward.

But the guilt women feel is not just imposed from the outside. The woman who has turned into a battle-ax may not necessarily like it. For those who could not live the role of submissive, nurturing woman there was only one other choice available: the role of shrew. Reversal of roles provides the escape valve all societies need in order to preserve a particular system of values, offering as it does a mode of behavior that can be understood, if not approved. For both the shrew and the supportive woman accept the idea that pleasing goes with weakness and subservience.

But being a shrew takes a terrible toll on the soul of a strong woman. The shrewish women I grew up among were always bitter and angry—desperately unhappy, even if they did "wear the pants" in the family. Their emotional and sexual needs were not being met, neither by their husbands nor by their children, for they had as little talent for mothering as they had for wifery. Yet these women had brains, energy, spirit, beauty—in another time, another context, they might have used their attributes to gain a more satisfying life.

If men really believed women to be inferior, they would not find it necessary to insist upon it so much, to preach the gospel of female subordination as the natural order of the universe. When exhortations and threats are not enough, men are not ashamed to resort to pleading.

A young director of a narcotics program, expressing the attitude of many black males, had this to say: "The only way an addict can be cured is through a woman.... The black man is ... hostile and even barbaric. Women have to understand that.... The only way a man can be a man is if a woman is a woman. A woman should not compete with a man, she should make him aware of what his capabilities are."

This man was not talking about women's weakness; quite the contrary. He was asking the woman to *choose* submission. In return he offered the opportunity of "saving" the man. A similar sentiment has been expressed by George Gilder, author of *Naked Nomads,* who warns that men turn into savages without the civilizing and nurturing influence of women, and that this spells "sexual suicide" for the race. Thus, it is the woman alone who has the power to grant rebirth, just as she alone has the power to give birth.

The "savior" role can seem very seductive indeed and may be one reason women have gone along so readily with the bargain sealed long ago: private power for public subservience. It is not just that women have chosen the lazy, easy way out—that we prefer to control and manipulate indirectly, as charged by Esther Vilar, a German woman attempting to discredit the women's liberation movement in her book, *The Manipulated Man.* Still, there is enough truth in her accusations to make us feel a twinge of shame at having sold our birthright for security, that proverbial mess of porridge. We feel guilty even though we cannot help ourselves, have been methodically conditioned to be just as we are, deep-down lazy and afraid and, at the same time, arrogant, in the secret knowledge of our hidden powers. It does not matter that they, the men, are lazy and afraid and arrogant too.

The truth is they are *both* right, the feminists who say women are exploited and abused by men, and those, like Esther Vilar, who claim that women exploit and manipulate men. In the existential reality of our lives, these two facts in no way cancel each other out but coexist. They offset each other in the same way as the myths of female power and female weakness. It is useless to assign blame. The situation has existed, in this circular way, for ages.

"Women don't change—any more than men do," wrote D. H. Lawrence in one of his essays.

> They only go through a rather regular series of phases. First slave, then obedient helpmeet, then respected spouse, then noble matron, then splendid woman and citizen; then finally, the independent female and modern girl.

There is something offensively smug and simplistic about Lawrence's analysis. But, again, there is more truth here than we might care to admit. What happens at the end of the independent-modern-female cycle? Back to slavery, of course. When the New Woman runs full tilt into the cichlid effect, she can give up on men altogether, or else espouse slavery again—a kind of involuntary emotional slavery so insidious and unconscious that it is difficult to make her see it and admit it.

In "saloon society," a certain kind of sexual equality has been operative for years. There are many cities where the local bar serves as a kind of club; people of similar interests and/or professions make a habit of meeting there almost every evening, to gossip and exchange information as well as to drink. The women "regulars" at these bars often get drunk, grow loud and boisterous, start fights, pick up men to bed for the night—in short, they are allowed to behave the way men do. At the same time, there is a strange combination of rapaciousness and abjectness in their relations with men.

A male friend of mine, commenting on this phenomenon, expressed surprise at the number of masochistic women that still seemed to be around. "I have a certain regard for some of these women, who are quite intelligent and talented," he said, "but I find it a little disgusting when they make a public display of what I consider slavishness."

We went on to talk about a woman we both knew, a talented musician. Her father and her brother, who are in the same field, have gotten all the breaks; she is just as good, if not better, but never received equal recognition or pay. She is righteously angry at the injustice of it, and will go on and on about that, to anyone who'll listen. But her scene with her men has always scandalized the most tolerant of her friends and acquaintances. We remembered her fierce defense of some guy who had run off with her money and used to slap her around all over the bar. She was ready to cut you to pieces if you put him down—absolutely ferocious. Hers is the psychology of the gun moll, the Angel Mama. And in fact, as a teen-ager, she did belong to a motorcycle gang.

"What amazes me is the guys," said my friend. "They know how to manipulate these women psychologically, and have made a career out of living this way. They're not men I'd seek out to have a drink with. But there seem to be enough women like that around so that the men can move from one to the other. Have you ever thought of talking about this to some of these women."

I told him I'd thought about it but was afraid I'd get a beer bottle broken over my head. I do not believe these women are masochistic so much as desperate. Not knowing quite what they're doing, or why, but trying to cope with emotions and circumstances and exigencies they don't really understand. Drinking helps. Not being introspective helps. You are not so aware of inconsistencies.

In actuality, the goddess and the slave are not really that different from each other. Like the Angel Mama, they are one and the same, opposite sides of the coin. A goddess who wishes to mate with a man must humble herself. She must give him to understand that, though her mere glance may strike terror into the hearts of other men, for *his* sake she will strip herself of all her power, be his servant and his slave, if only he will return her love.

A woman I know was telling me about the "strange" behavior of her nineteen-year-old daughter. Brought up to be proud and free by progressive-minded parents, this intelligent, attractive girl waits on her boyfriend "hand and foot"—fusses over him, watches what he eats, indulges his whims, defends his bad habits, and in general "treats him like a pasha," as the nonplused mother puts it. The most puzzling part of the story is that the young woman is not really very deeply involved. There are too many things she wants to do before tying in seriously with one man, and her mother is sure she has no thoughts of marriage or other long-term alliance. He is merely the boyfriend of the moment. How then account for what looks to the mother like a return to the old female subservience? Nothing in the girl's upbringing, let alone the spirit of the times, would seem to warrant such regression.

And this story does not represent an isolated instance. So far from pressuring their men to share the housework or help in the kitchen, many young women today delight in poring over recipes and learning to make soups and cakes from scratch. They make sure the man they fancy has clean socks and underwear; they massage his neck when he's tense, listen sympathetically to his complaints and problems. The young men, for their part, seem to accept all this as their due. With liberation in the air, why are so many young women trying to turn back the clock?

The fact is very young women often have not personally experienced oppression at the hands of men. They grew up believing they had plenty of options, in career or life style, and expecting to stand on their own feet, financially and psychologically. The outrage of the militant feminists must seem a bit on the abstract side to them; the grievances are much more deeply felt by women in their thirties and forties, who've experienced them at first hand. Not that the younger woman doesn't appreciate how fortunate she is to be living at a time when there are so many possibilities open to her. At the same time, she has a vague sense of loss —a feeling that a certain coldness, a kind of emotional sterility are involved in the ideals of women's liberation.

When the pendulum has swung too far in one direction,

we try to swing it back the other way, so as to maintain a balance. This attempt to deal with emotional future shock accounts for the prevalence of nostalgia, the current glorification of the past—and the recent past at that—in literature, film, and fashion. Nostalgia for romance—an unwillingness to forgo the quickening and glamour of the Zap, which has formed such an important part of our social and psychological heritage—seems to be at the root of what one man has called the New Masochism—one possible response to the cichlid effect and the New Impotence.

However, the term "masochism" is misleading. The young women of today cater to their men not because they have to but because they want to, and there is no reason to assume they are suffering. What's more, it is not with *all* men that they act in this self-abnegating way but only with the men they have set their hearts on. For the New Woman, the man in her life has only one purpose and function—he is a *love* object, first, foremost, and last. Love objects, whatever their sex, exist to be pampered and petted. Men are being treated with the kind of affectionate indulgence women have traditionally shown toward their children—especially their sons.

This doting on the man of one's choice may well go hand in hand with mistrust of, and contempt for, men in general. (It is not unlike those instances, quite common in the past, of a man's humbling himself to please a beloved wife, mistress, or daughter. It is certain that man never doubted his intrinsic superiority over women, even over the women who held him emotionally in thrall.) Today's women are being indulgent and protective toward men they feel to be essentially vulnerable, and in need of support. For man is no longer the hunter, woman the prey who yields, willingly or otherwise, to a superior force. In fact, we may be on our way, in some areas, to reverting to matriarchal types of societies. Such societies have existed for some time, in big-city ghettos and the Virgin Islands—in cultures all over Africa, Asia, South America and the South Seas—areas where opportunities for men to exert power in the world are severely limited, and women represent the stable element. If men have not exactly become the weaker sex, their ascendancy has certainly been put in question.

Over the ages, the male ego has been blown up to such proportions that now it seems the merest pinprick is enough to puncture the balloon. As one woman remarked, "Who wants to be left with a crumpled balloon?" Of course, the ego couldn't go on being inflated indefinitely, even with all the social support and the collusion of women. Something had to give. And give it did—is, in fact, still giving—and the casualties are enormous. Many confused and terrified men are dropping out, and falling by the wayside.

Let them fall, the militant feminists might say. But most women, even of feminist persuasion, don't feel that way. They have a tremendous psychic stake in passionate, romantic man-woman love, even if the ideals of permanence, family, and a life shared on all fronts no longer form an essential part of the picture. Of course, some women still believe they can have it *all* ways—expecting the man to be lover, husband, father, provider, friend—thereby letting themselves in for a lot of disappointment and grief.

But other women know exactly where things stand, even if they are not fully conscious of this knowledge. Though they are hooked on the Zap, they are not quite so encircled by the men they love. They know they are strong, and able to take care of business as well as, if not better than, the man. Thus they can afford to be generous and not make demands that are too heavy. The woman needs the man to fill the gap in her emotional life, and though she may cook him gourmet meals, take home his laundry, and endlessly massage his delicate, aching ego, she isn't so likely to consult him about major life decisions. If she does ask his advice on questions of career or education, family matters or legal problems, chances are she will make up her own mind in the end. And when the time comes, she will go her own way, leaving the man behind if need be.

Watching the young women in their calico dresses, making granola and patching their men's jeans, it may seem as if nothing has really changed. But there *is* this crucial difference: the men are sons and lovers, not husbands and fathers. For the woman, it is no longer a question of survival but of choice. No one is forcing her to give more than she gets. If she can accept the mother-son type of love, which seems to be a trend of the times, and forget what the psychoanalysts say, then she need not feel guilty or put-upon. There are many ways to love, and this one has advantages as well as drawbacks. It allows the woman a large measure of inner freedom and control over her own life.

The impulse to please someone we care for is very powerful. It starts to feel wrong only if the impulse comes out of fear and need, rather than generosity of spirit.

"If a woman is not subservient in *any* way, she's in trouble," observed one woman. "Because of the bind the men are in, the old-fashioned kind of woman turns them off. Who wants someone who's clingy and makes endless demands? Of course they want an intelligent, independent woman. The only trouble is they can't *make* it with her— unless, though she's tough as nails in the outside world, when she comes home it's Sweetie, what would you like to eat? and plumping a pillow for his back. And that's just what most of the career women I know are doing."

Women have wanted public power, public equality. We are getting what we wanted, slowly but inexorably. And just as inexorably we are losing the considerable private power we wielded with our food and our children and our sex. Food and sex may no longer be bartered, they have lost their leverage. And children are at best a personal indulgence.

The leaders of women's liberation surely did not foresee these developments; neither the cichlid effect nor the New Masochism have been officially recognized. But some awareness of these phenomena may be one reason the lesbian banner has been raised so high. Don't sleep with men, they warn us. If you sleep with your "oppressor," it can only end in grief. The "oppression," however, for many of us today might well be imposed from within, rather than without, a matter of our own needs and choices.

But all the ideology in the world cannot prevent those of us who are inclined that way from falling in love with men. That fire in the heart and loins—if it flares only with a man and not a woman, what is there to do? Oh yes, we want freedom and equality. We want peace with honor. But above all, we want *love*—and, of course, the sexual fulfillment that is our due.

Why not ask for more?

3
Romance Is a Dance

It might be argued that only those who are open to the experience of loneliness can know the true poignancy and joy of love. There are people who do not allow themselves to be lonely. They are very social, always surrounded by others, forever in "relationships." Since they do not *feel* loneliness, it doesn't exist for them. It is quite possible that love does not exist for them either.

Then there are people who are born with a certain predisposition toward solitude. They may be shy and withdrawn, or boisterous and full of bravura, but you can spot them—a sadness, a distance comes into their eyes at the most unexpected moments. If this predisposition hardens into alienation and is felt as agony, the fault lies as much with the values of our society as with the individuals themselves. It is shameful and "sick" to be lonely, a condition that must be medicated and cured. In former times, in other cultures, this quality of inner reserve was respected, if not admired; from such humans came artists and inventors, poets and philosophers, prophets and saints. Even in our own history, the solitary western hero who scorns civilization and the companionship of family and friends—this lonely existential hero who is often paranoid and criminal to boot—still has the power to fire the youthful imagination. How to square this with the dictum: "Relate and Be Happy?"

A woman is taught to view loneliness as failure. While a man might seek a solitary path and go to meditate upon a mountain, without pity or censure from the world, a woman has to fight not only social pressures, but the powerful conditioning that has enjoined upon her, since childhood, the need for emotional fulfillment through others. People who need people are not really the luckiest people in the world, yet many women still believe this drivel, despite the evidence all around them.

Men seem to find it easier to accept a basic solitude. Keeping busy, fighting and striving, getting echoes back from the world at large, all help to make the condition tolerable—perhaps even constructive. When women worked hard all their lives and had many children, their fate was certainly not enviable, but chances are they had neither the time nor the opportunity to brood about being lonely and unloved. But once the notion took firm root in their minds, it grew into a veritable monster of fierce and painful longing.

This longing for romance, the addiction to love-sex, cannot be reasoned away. It can only be repressed or transcended. A cause or a religion might provide a satisfactory substitute, but a career is not likely to, and neither are children. Though they may help to build a life for a woman, frequently career or children only make the emotional hunger more poignant. Even a steady, unromantic husband may not help—married women are notoriously prone to the familiar vague ache and yearning.

"I remember love's enchantments" muses the housewife heroine of Fay Weldon's novel, *Female Friends*.

> Sometimes something happens, like the sun across the garden in the morning, or a song, or a smell, or the touch of a hand—and the body remembers

what love was like, and the soul lifts itself up,
certain once again in the knowledge of its creator;
and the whole self trembles again in the memory
of that elation, which once so transfigured our
poor obsessed bodies, our poor possessed minds.

"It did us no good," she adds. But whether love has done
us good or not, we remember its enchantments, when we
are not under its sway, with an emotion that is almost
mystical, almost religious, even if overlaid with a thin
veneer of fashionable cynicism.

Is there nothing unalterable about the female obsession
with romance? Women in the past, women in other parts of
the world seemed to manage, and manage still, to live quite
well without. But in our culture, the craving has been in-
jected into our blood at so early an age, in such concentrated
doses, that if we are deprived for any length of time we begin
to wither, to die inside. Rather than that, we will do *anything*—even for the precarious "freshening" that a night
of good sex can bring, or even the temporary reassurance
that a night of uninspired sex can bring, if only we can find
some warmth of touch, some affection.

But a night in bed often brings neither freshening nor
reassurance, only more confusion, greater longing. Screw-
ing around messes up your mind and your body responses.
There's this hole in your soul, and no amount of cock is
going to fill it.

What happens then is that you spend a lot of time lying
around in a funk, concocting endless romantic-erotic day-
dreams, the way you did when you were a kid. The contents
of my own fantasies have changed considerably since I was
fourteen, but their essential nature hasn't: in them I strive
to play the Great Game, so beautifully, so truly, that nobody
loses. My partner and I surmount all the pitfalls, triumph
over all the demons, and stay in synch all the time—not
glued together, in old tango style, but watching each other,
taking cues from each other, adding to one another's dance.
These fancies come upon me like attacks of flu, leaving me
drained and lethargic and depressed. Doctor, I have this

recurrent dream: I shall find someone to love and live happily ever after.

Dreams aside, we know that to live in a state of love is not easy. Someone is forever squatting inside your head, monitoring every move. You never think of buying anything for yourself without wondering, Will he like it? An incident in the street or in the office is not savored but instantly reduced to anecdote, for dishing up to your loved one at home. Of course, some people would find nothing wrong with such "sharing." And others might rebel by doing something their partner *doesn't* like, quite deliberately and spitefully, rather than because they really want to do it. Either way, they are not free agents. For many people this kind of possession is a hardship—it doesn't allow enough inner space for the personality to unfold according to its inner bent. For an ever-larger number of women, the great need for romance is pitted against a growing impatience, an increasing intolerance for all the mind-fucking that goes on in the name of love.

I believe the problem lies in the phenomenon of falling in love itself and cannot be blamed on the war between the sexes. This conclusion was borne out by the homosexuals I talked with. They seemed to be having just as much trouble with love as anyone else—perhaps more, for they have even less tradition to fall back on, and place even greater weight on the love affair as an end in itself. Both male and female homosexuals admitted to being tossed between joy and sorrow, depending on the moods of the beloved, and to feeling incomplete without that special someone to care for. Homosexual men, unlike straight men, seem to be as hung up on love as women are.

It seems that when love, and even pleasure, are pursued simply for their own sakes, they often fail to provide full satisfaction. Only when attraction is based not exclusively on some projected fantasy but on some common purpose is there any hope that it will grow into enduring love.

Love seems to work best when it is a by-product of something that transcends the "relationship" itself, such as dedication to a cause, a belief, a work project, or even a new life style. At one time, the raising of children, the demands of family and clan provided strong enough cement to bind a couple together—that and the weight of the belief that marriage was for life. Today, families are scattered, and children are no longer a necessity for survival; consequently, they tend to be a liability in a union based on romantic love. Work seems to be a good common purpose—the Curies come to mind and, more recently, Masters and Johnson. The best example for me, because they are not married or even living together but have loved each other for more than a quarter of a century, are Simone de Beauvoir and Jean-Paul Sartre.

Having some other primary goal, we need not make such heavy demands on our partners. For when we *must* have something, we are already in trouble. As money comes easily to the rich, so love comes more readily to those who are not forever seeking it, who give off those ineffable vibes of self-containment, which have nothing to do with the outward trappings of liberation and cannot be faked. "Clutching is the surest way to murder love," says May Sarton in *Journal of a Solitude,* "as if it were a kitten, not to be squeezed so hard, or a flower to fade in a tight hand."

Admittedly, it is difficult to care but not care too much— to stay open and potent in loving and at the same time maintain one's own center; and, when the time comes, to let go with grace and dignity, absorbing the hurt without resistance, so it will pass more quickly, and, above all, not taking it so *personally* . . . remembering that *everybody,* regardless of merit, has been hurt, rejected, betrayed—Christ, Cleopatra, and even Elizabeth Taylor. The death of love is painful, but it can be borne without shame, humiliation, or self-loathing, provided we can deprogram ourselves from the wounded-ego bit: "How dare he do this to me?" or the other side of the coin, self-pity: "Why are guys always doing this to me?"

Most of our woes come from being unable to accept things as they really are. What if, in our secret hearts, we are relieved to be rid of the creep, and know it's the best thing that could have happened? He *jilted* us, didn't he? So we respond with Pavlovian reflex pain, unwilling to accept that we cannot lose what we never possessed. We find it hard to let go, of hate if it cannot be love, for hate, too, is a bond and a connection. What if we should lose our hatreds, along with our loves, and fall into the emptiness of freedom? For many, this represents the ultimate terror.

People have told me, smiling a little defensively, that I am pessimistic. In terms of the accepted views of how love relations *should* be—according to either traditional concepts or the radical-revolutionary bias of the moment—I am indeed pessimistic about real-life people ever fitting into those narrow slots. But I am optimistic about the possibility of revising our attitudes and our goals; of sharpening our awareness so that we may rid ourselves of destructive habits of thinking and feeling. I even believe it is possible to learn to *enjoy* variety and complexity, the irrational, unpredictable, and *funny* things that can happen between human beings involved in the explosive combinations, or permutations, of love and sex.

"The serious problems of life are never fully solved," said Carl Gustav Jung.

> If they should appear to be so it is a sure sign that something has been lost. The meaning and purpose of a problem seem to lie not in its solution but in our working on it incessantly. This alone prevents us from stultification and putrefaction.

The striving toward growth and development we call liberation involves a day-to-day struggle. But this struggle can be creative, full of exciting possibilities, provided our efforts are directed not toward changing events—"working" on a relationship, or making a partner "come around"

—but toward altering our own demands and expectations. The problems of love, and the difficulties of sex, may never be solved. But we may perhaps learn to deal with them, without despair—or undue hope.

sex

1
Sex and Sociability
or Everything You've Read About Sex and Ought to Forget

Instant Sex, a major tenet of the sexual revolution and the new morality it engendered, is based on the principle that sex is a shortcut to intimacy. The idea is to "get that out of the way," as one young man put it. I asked him what happens once you get it out of the way. "Then," he said, "whatever the possibilities are, they are." He admitted that he was, at the outset, mostly interested in the sex as an expression of acceptance by the woman. Several other men also told me they needed this kind of "reassurance" before anything further could happen.

At the same time, these men—and most of the people I talked with—agreed that sex has a tendency to "fuck up" friendship. It "shouldn't" be that way, but apparently that is the case—for homosexuals as well as for heterosexuals. I shall deal with this phenomenon more thoroughly in the chapter on friendship; here, suffice it to say that, so far from being a shortcut to intimacy, sex often cuts short the chances of forming a close liaison if the people get into it before they feel sufficiently comfortable with each other.

Few budding friendships survive the failure of sex, the well-established ones may well do so. For that matter, few budding friendships survive the success of sex, for then the union usually turns into something else. The couple may get involved in power plays, with sex as weapon and prize, and never come to know one another at all.

As in most revolutionary credos, there is a lot of wishful thinking behind the new sexual ethos. We are supposed to be such high-powered bundles of erotic TNT that if any and all sexual tension is not immediately discharged, we are expected to explode ... or else become hopeless neurotics. In this swing of the pendulum to the opposite extreme of puritanism, the new mythology, as usual, ignores the evidence: with all our sexual freedom, we are more violent, destructive, and anxiety-ridden than ever.

As a matter of plain fact, instant, overwhelming mutual attractions are relatively rare, and the following double bind is far more typical of what actually happens: Say a man and a woman have just met. They would like to get better acquainted, but they can no longer stay at the bar or at the party, or wherever. So they decide to continue their conversation at one or the other's house. By then it is usually late, and soon there comes the point where both are tired—it's time for bed. Invariably, the man feels compelled to make a sexual overture. Even if neither party is really turned on, the sexual question must be raised—to prove his manhood as well as her desirability. The woman may know from sad experience (and maybe the man does too) that without true desire, which might come with a deepening of intimacy and trust, the sex won't be any good. Impossible for her to say, "Not now, but maybe later." The man will be indignant, contemptuous—that's what women *used* to say, wasn't it, stalling for time and playing their teasing games? Though he may secretly share the woman's misgivings, and even be relieved at her refusal, his ego is at stake and he invariably feels, or acts, offended.

Even if she succeeds in explaining her feelings and he says he understands—promises to call, and maybe even means it—by the next night he may have met someone who *does* sleep with him right away. Whether or not the sex is all that great, his attention has been diverted and the impact of meeting the first woman is gone. So what she feared happened anyway: she didn't have sex with him right off, and so will never see him again. Of course, if she does have sex with him and it's lousy, she may also never see him again, and feel ripped-off in the bargain. In effect, she's damned if she does, and damned if she doesn't.

Nor is it simply a matter of the woman being, once again, used and put-upon; quite often, the situation is reversed. A number of men I talked with complained that if they want to talk to a woman they find interesting, if not particularly desirable, she presupposes a sexual intention, and if they don't ask for her phone number or to take her home, she is offended. (It doesn't make any difference whether or not she really wants the man—the important thing is that he want *her*.)

One man told me what he quite often does is *take* the woman home, whether he feels like it or not. "Have you ever wound up in bed with someone," he asked, "simply because neither of you knew how to end it short of that without seeming to put the other down?"

Sure I have, and so have most of the people I know. With women, the social imperative to please frequently takes the form of going to bed with men so as "not to hurt their feelings." At a certain point, it becomes "too much trouble to say no," as one veteran of the compliant school phrased it. That most exasperating of questions, "Why not?" epitomizes the new sexual morality with its "thou shalt" commandments. If it is not only our right but our *duty* to fuck, then we must account for the absence of desire. If we are not particularly turned on by that many people, it means we are unliberated, hung-up, sick. We had better seek professional help forthwith.

"You can be attracted to anybody you like," said the young man who liked to get it out of the way. "People are responsible for the way they look, and if they're nice enough to like, they're nice enough to fuck."

Under the pressure of this unwritten code, the woman

can think of no "good" reason for refusing (it always amazes me how a man can want a woman, *desperately*—for half an hour). Fear of pregnancy has ceased to be a valid reason, and it never occurs to the woman that the question, if any, should be, "Why yes?" So she rationalizes . . . it's no big deal after all, and she really can't get out of it gracefully.

But her altruism is only apparent. What the woman hopes to gain by the sexual exchange is acceptance. If she says no, the man will reject her, fail to be her friend—maybe even spread the word that she's an uptight bitch. For if, in the past, a woman's status and self-esteem depended on *not* doing it, today they depend on *doing* it, and a girl who doesn't put out can kiss popularity good-by.

Since the original momentum of the sexual revolution is still carrying hard-core pornography into Middle America, and there is more nudity and more explicit sex than ever to be found in films, books, and magazines generally, one might be tempted to conclude that reports of its demise (the *Village Voice* ran a humorous obituary on the sexual revolution) are premature to say the least. However, the apparent health of the porn business may be as deceptive as the roses in the cheeks of the consumptive. Overexposure is always lethal in the long run—and often in the short run too.

If you repress something, you merely drive it underground, there to flourish or fester, but in any case, to survive. But an overdose is quick, efficient, and deadly. While guilt and secrecy might even lend an extra thrill to the proceedings, as witnessed by the flowering of pornography and perversity in the Age of Victoria, the night-and-day bombardment of erotically charged words and images has had the opposite effect; when the message in the media always comes down to S-E-X, the result can only be sensory overload.

You get up in the morning and turn on the radio: to the accompaniment of throbbing drums and guitar, a voice moons about how her kisses thrill him. In the street you

pass a newsstand: people in provocative states of near un-
dress leer at you suggestively from the covers of various
periodicals. In the subway: the ad shows a seductive blonde
with a come-hither look who asks if you've had any lately.
It's not even nine o'clock in the morning and already you've
been exposed to more explicit sexual stimuli than your
grandparents encountered in a lifetime. Small wonder that,
after a time, a kind of numbness sets in. We develop a ho-
hum attitude, if not downright disenchantment, and we
begin to wonder, Do we need vitamins? Are we getting old?

Part of our American heritage is the belief that we can
legislate improvements in human nature. The movement for
sexual freedom, like so many others, was founded on this
belief—it also foundered on it. Though the media tried to
force the new sexuality deep down our throats, so to speak,
this did not mean we were ready to digest it.

Many people have found the prospect of real sexual freedom terrifying in the extreme. Like those prisoners who
are psychologically unable to deal with living free and
promptly wind up in the safety of another jail, a lot of folks
who believe themselves to be sexually liberated (because
they *do* it all the time) in reality have become boxed into
attitudes and behavior that inhibit the joyful expression of
their sexuality as much as, if not more than, the puritanism
they congratulate themselves on having overcome.

In the bad old days, sex was either a natural need or a
sacrament—even when it became a sin, no one doubted that
it was exciting. About the best that can be said for sex these
days is that it is Fun, and that overinflated Mad Ave word,
suggestive of Disneyland and home hair-coloring kits, almost precludes the possibility that sex can be something
other, or more, than fun. To become part of the Good Life,
sex had to be denied its power—reduced to the lowest
common denominator, so it could become available to the
greatest number of people. Sex may be healthy, keep you
youthful and socially in the swing—it may be fun. But
where's the urgency, the magic, the madness? No matter
how we try to soup it up with various exotica, with multiple
partners and positions—the thrill is going . . . is almost gone.

And we feel cheated. Is this what we fought and won the sexual revolution for?

The doing-it-more-and-enjoying-it-less syndrome is in large part the result of going to bed with people for reasons that have nothing to do with sex. In some circles, people fuck or swing the way they would play tennis or golf, as a kind of social credit card. This "recreational" sex is "very demanding," even its champion, Dr. David Reuben admits. The reason it is so demanding is that it has to conform to the standards set by the sexperts. No longer are we permitted to have any old sex, a private matter between ourselves and our partners. The stakes are too high; they involve not only our physical and mental health, but also our social life and reputation. With performances carefully clocked, it's hard to have fun when you're constantly keeping score and worrying about measuring up.

The pressure to conform to certain "norms," along with the welter of statistics, conjecture, myth, dogma, and just plain wishful thinking that passes for sex information, has created a new Age of Sexual Anxiety that makes the old one seem positively benign. We dare not admit to our fears, our inadequacies. It is easier to drop out of the sexual Olympics altogether. When so many young men and women in their physical prime are forgoing the sex games in favor of hard drugs, or some currently popular political or religious movement, it's time to admit there's something amiss in our sexual utopia. For these dropouts include many people who *do* have their act together in the sack and are confident of their performance, but who find—like that spokesman for the libido on the loose, Mick Jagger—that they can get no satisfaction. Unlike the sexperts, they know better than to equate orgasm with satisfaction.

For some people, of course, there is a lot of satisfaction to be found in conquest. Sex as a form of power has been around for a long time, and winning is the point of the game. There are men who will climb a woman because, like the mountain, she is *there*. But the conquering hero's need to be in control makes it hard for him to relax and enjoy himself. First, he has to overcome the woman's resistance and "get it" from her, and then he has to worry about extricating himself from any consequent demands or expectations she might have.

Such considerations are inimical to pleasure, and there is a growing unease, a strong suspicion that there might be better ways than sexual conquest to achieve ego gratification. This idea was expressed by Boris, a twenty-eight-year-old former advertising man. Recently divorced, Boris is very attached to his five-year-old daughter, who spends most weekends with him. He is the only father who volunteers time to serve in the community day-care center, a fact which he claims is turning all the other fathers in the neighborhood against him, since their wives are always holding him up as an example. At the time of our talk, Boris was in a men's consciousness-raising group and given to breast-beating about his residual chauvinism.

"I always relate differently after sex," he said. "Sometimes better, sometimes not, but it always makes a difference. If I like a woman, the sexual thing always crosses my mind: What's she like in bed? How will I be with her in bed? A thought just came to me: Had we, at some point previously, had sex and then set out to have this conversation, would I be acting differently, talking differently? I suspect I would.

"That's a real *macho* trip and I feel guilty because the woman seems more vulnerable in the situation. Before sex, the woman more or less has power; she has something I want. After sex, I somehow feel I got something, in the sense that I took something away from her, and the woman usually feels more clingy. I've found this to be fairly general with men . . . they've scored with the chick, done their man thing; the mystery is gone, and the relationship is at a very precarious point. It depends on how strong the conquest thing is in the man, but that may have been the sole basis for the encounter, even if he told himself he really liked her. Too many times, I've realized—tricked myself, if you like—that that's all *I* really wanted. I did it and that was it."

The use of sex for power, as well as profit, is not confined to men, however. It has been part of female psychological warfare since antiquity. Liberation notwithstanding, the mentality of the prostitute is still very much with us, and it is by no means confined to women who earn their living that way. The heroine of the anonymously-authored book *Groupie* describes her triumph on leaving a night club with a well-known rock star, so everyone could see how she had "pulled" him, even though the sex, when they finally got around to it, was both perfunctory and degrading. The "star fucker" is more interested in the prestige of the man she beds or weds than anything else about him. I've heard women say, "I'm going out with this physicist (eye surgeon, concert pianist)," only to learn, later on, that the gentleman in question was a sadist, a pathological liar, and chronically impotent.

By far the most common reason for having sex (apart from a purely physiological urge) is a particular kind of loneliness—a hunger for close physical contact. In America, where all touch is suspect and even the handshake has become obsolete, the only way an adult can be held and cuddled is in a sexual context. Everyone I talked with admitted going to bed with someone just to be next to a warm body. This is one of the great benefits of marriage or its equivalent; you may still fall asleep with your arms around each other long after desire has fled your bed.

But for those who live alone, it is not easy to wait for a genuine attraction. It may take a while—sometimes a *long* while—and in the meantime, you begin to feel a little subhuman. After a few weeks or months, depending on your tolerance, you may begin to wonder if the machinery still works. Then it seems as if everybody else is out there doing it, having a marvelous time (though you may know better, deep down, as they say) and you feel monumentally deprived. It's affection you crave, but it comes on as sex, so you hop into bed with the first likely prospect. And more likely than not, you wind up more frustrated than you were before.

Buddy, who admires the optimism of women, calls it "bed-hoping." What do people hope for, I asked him. "That something is going to come of it," he replied, "whether it's love, or an orgasm, or a job, or merely something different. These people who hop into bed at the drop of an innuendo ... they are the eternal optimists."

I asked Buddy why intelligent, sensitive men insist on going through with sex, and even put on pressure, when they know the woman is not really interested. "I've known a woman was going to bed with me out of *revenge*, to get back at her old man, and I *still* went through with it," he said. "The man fears the woman will say he couldn't cut the mustard. Also, we've been programed to believe anything you start, you finish. Look at what goes on in the theater! They'll invest twenty thousand dollars in a play, and they see it's a dog, but they go on with it—they even put more money into it. Same as with sex, there's always the hope against hope that by some miracle, when we finally get into it, it's going to work."

Hope goes hand in hand with illusion. "There's this deceptive quality to the male ego," another man told me. "You might know that you are being, let us say, endured, but you are quite capable of deluding yourself into believing the woman is merely putting up a pretense of not wanting it. Who could fail to want me as I perform this marvelous feat?"

If men and women both hope the sex is going to "work," that ambiguous term may well mean different things to them. "Lots of us went to bed with men we weren't really attracted to," said New Zealand–bound Renata, "because a man's sexuality is such that a woman can change her mind if he turns out to be a magnificent lover and she's had an orgasm."

Renata's sophistication does not make her immune to the peculiar blindness of bed-hoping. Was it entirely a matter of the man's technique whether or not she had an orgasm, I asked. Of course not, she admitted. What she really needed was a sense of security—to know the man was going to be there the next day, and the next, so she could build around him sexually, and he around her. Then there were no problems. "I don't go to bed with men just to have an orgasm," she explained. "But I may sleep with someone I don't really expect to have a relationship with; it's pleasant, the coming together, the closeness, and maybe I'll come, and maybe something will come of it. Usually, nothing has come of it."

I suggested it might be somewhat unrealistic to expect something really good to come of an experience you approach in such a lukewarm mood. "But everybody does," said Renata. "You don't necessarily expect that anything great is going to happen. Men have been going to bed with women for centuries and having orgasms, but it's the rare woman who can come in a night's adventure."

Whether or not this is generally true, Renata's plight points up the circular quality of the sexual worry. The man is concerned about his prowess and/or performance, the woman about having an orgasm. By their very nature, these anxieties tend to be self-fulfilling prophesies, bringing about the very failures that are being feared.

The belief that woman's pleasure is largely a function of the man's performance lays a heavy burden on him, at the same time as it absolves her of equal responsibility. But it was Masters and Johnson who pointed out in their most recent book, *The Pleasure Bond* (intended, no doubt, to correct some of the wrong conclusions drawn from their earlier works), that there is no way one individual can assume responsibility for another's natural physical processes—no way a man can "give" a woman an orgasm, or a woman can provide a man with an ejaculation.

Women must beware of making the mistake men have made in the past, of seeing sex as a service to be rendered. If men once tended to view the female as a receptacle, today's women are likely to think of the male as an instrument, according to Masters and Johnson.

Many women are not heeding this warning, however, and it is not an uncommon practice among certain "hip" women to talk about the men they sleep with, grading and giving out points. Renata and others indignantly rejected the suggestion that there might be a lot of hostility involved in this practice. After all, men have been talking about women this way for centuries, they said defensively. When I pointed out the obvious—that two wrongs don't make a right— Renata admitted that what might be involved is a form of bragging, or homosexual titillation (certainly it isn't *information*, and it doesn't take much experimenting to learn that one woman's great lay is another woman's ho-hum). In any case, said Renata, this kind of talk wasn't very important.

Men don't agree, however, and tend to resent such talk, even when the report card is good. These feelings were strongly expressed by Danny, who spent much of his youth on the road, dropped-out and hirsute, pushing pot and visiting communes. At the age of thirty-three, he has so far avoided marriage or facsimiles thereof, one reason being that his father told him the meaning and worth of a man was to work hard all his life to support his family.

Danny described an incident at a party given by a former girlfriend: "These two women kept staring at me," he said. "They were grinning and looking at my crotch. Finally one of them says, 'You're Danny, aren't you. I understand you're dynamite in bed.' I got really pissed off. 'What is this shit?' I said. 'It depends on who I'm *with* whether or not I'm dynamite in bed. Sometimes I'm really lousy, like when I'm with a woman I don't really dig. I get in and out as fast as possible.' "

I wondered why he went to bed with women he didn't really dig. "Sometimes it's loneliness," he said. "Or else it's boredom. She's there and willing, and what else have I got to do tonight?" Danny admitted this attitude was a hangover from the psychology of scarcity, of get-it-while-you-can. He also pointed out that, while it was still relatively acceptable for a woman to say no, for a man to say no was the consummate insult. "What are you going to say? 'I have a headache, dear? I got my period?' A man is supposed to be ever-ready, like the battery."

It is true that hell hath no fury like a woman spurned by a man she desires, though she may complain bitterly about being a sex object when she's not turned on. Once I was sitting with a group of women at a table in our favorite pub. A man we all knew walked by and one of the women said, "He's supposed to be such a great stud. He can't even get it up!" Some of us had been his lovers, and we exchanged amused and pitying glances, but said nothing to the woman who was so blinded by her rage she didn't realize she was treading on very thin ice. For a man will almost always go to bed with a woman who asks him, or indicates strongly enough that she wants him to. Not only is his male ego at stake, and he has the bed-hope that it's going to work out fine, but he knows it's *really* going to hurt the woman's feelings if he refuses, much more so than if he goes home with her and then makes his excuses—drank too much, too stoned—allowing her the solace of pity and contempt for the poor, impotent bastard.

Not only do people have sex when they don't really want to, they are wont to engage in sexual acts they don't really enjoy. We are expected to do certain things, and if we don't, what will our partners think? Certain practices have become so *de rigueur* they are performed almost as a ritual, whether or not we feel like doing that particular thing at that particular moment. "I can always tell when a woman is really into it [fellatio] and when she isn't," said Danny. "And I've said, 'Please stop, because it's only going to bring you down and bring me down.' "

Women also have told me they could always tell the difference between duty and pleasure and would prefer to do without cunnilingus if their partner didn't really like what he was doing. Danny pointed out, however, that one might have to overcome an initial reluctance before one learned to love it. "For many men, cunnilingus is an acquired taste," he said. "Like Greek olives."

The problem is one of communication. For all the ease and frequency with which we indulge in sex, we are notoriously closemouthed in bed. Of course, communication doesn't involve just talking, and talk is not necessarily communication. However, it seems surprisingly difficult to say, on the one hand, please don't (men, especially, get quite upset at the suggestion that there's something they're not doing right), and on the other hand, let me keep trying, I want to learn. People tend to conceal their true sexual feelings for fear these may be emotionally unappealing to their partners, according to Masters and Johnson. The openness and willingness to send and receive messages, both verbal and nonverbal, requires a considerable amount of trust, for in the sexual sphere we continue to be extremely vulnerable.

Sometimes, it's not so much a matter of sexual inhibition as of social shyness and tact. If you've invited someone into your home and bed, it seems as rude to comment on that person's sexual technique as it would be to criticize a guest's table manners. It is assumed, after all, that everyone over the age of fifteen knows everything there is to know about sex.

There are a lot of people who, having read the sexperts, are trying to do a lot of things for which they have no real aptitude or liking. There have *always* been people who liked to swing, who were bisexual, or polymorphous perverse, or whatever, before there were names and labels for such behavior. I suspect that if we were to follow up on the people who are genuinely enjoying the new sex styles and feeling no ill side effects, we might discover the percentage to be not much larger than it was before.

In our achievement-oriented culture, we don't like to admit that technique might not be the real issue. The mood and feeling of a sexual encounter involve intangibles that are difficult to discuss. *Après faire l'amour, l'homme est triste,* say the French. Quite often, the man is not only sad, but unaccountably angry. He withdraws, appearing to reject the woman, who is feeling clingy out of the same mysterious disappointment—the failure of even "successful" sex to leave her feeling happy and satisfied. I've noticed this strange irritation in myself, as well as in the man, and wondered why, when everything went smoothly enough, and we both came.

The myth of the Big Orgasm in the Sky began with the resexualization of the female body, which constitutes one of the major cultural upheavals of this century. Ironically, the leaders were not the feminists but the marriage-manual writers. "In the beginning of this movement, sex was still a man's game, a benign master conferring a grace upon a subservient," writes Dr. Jessie Bernard, in *The Sex Game*.

> But little by little it was learned ... women could outperform men. The fifteenth century had known this. Imperial Rome had undoubtedly known. Contributors to the great Hebrew literature had known. But the nineteenth century had not known. Now the twentieth century did ... [and] there developed a veritable cult of orgasm. Women came to expect, even demand, sexual gratification on equal terms. It became practically a civil right.

More than a civil right, it became a sociosexual must. Not to produce the vaunted spasm is, for a woman, a failure akin to impotence. Beyond her own disappointment, she is disgraced in the eyes of her partner, who presumably has done all the prescribed things for the prescribed length of time. He asks questions such as, "Don't you ever come?" Or more sympathetically, "What makes you come?"—thinking there might be some offbeat button he has neglected to push. And one may want to say (though one never does), "I know you were working away, doing this and that, but as for any real connection with *me*, you might as well have been on Mars. Would you believe I've come with others in a few minutes, and without any frills?"

How to explain that it isn't a matter of any particular act or position or time span but of a certain kind of touch ... a certain *feeling*. Since this sort of remark sets a lot of

men's teeth on edge, let me hasten to say that the feeling I
refer to is not romantic or emotional. It is a *sexual* feeling—
a certain mood that allows you to tune in profoundly to
the forces that are engaging your body and your psyche . . .
a sense that your partner is to be trusted (in the sexual
sphere, if not elsewhere) to pick up on your signals so you
can let it all hang out, without self-consciousness or effort.

"Working" at achieving an orgasm is not unlike working
at love—often, the harder you or your partner work, the
less gratifying the results. For we are dealing with sex in a
vacuum, pulling it out of context from the rest of our lives.
The work ethic treats sex as something in and of itself, a
skill to be practiced and improved, leaving out of consideration the emotional factors that are responsible for most
sexual failures—suppressed resentment, unhappiness, anxiety.

Even if, after much hard work, you *do* achieve a climax,
it may not be very pleasurable. Marco Vassi describes it in
one of his erotic novels: "He gave a grunt like someone
having a splinter pulled. It was an orgasm of relief." Since
most men are aware that some orgasms are scarcely worth
the bother, why is the question of sexual fulfillment still
being put in terms of arithmetic—how often, how long, how
many times? Dr. Reuben actually has it clocked: how many
pelvic thrusts it takes to bring a woman to orgasm (somewhere between thirty and forty). You may laugh, but it is
amazing how many people prefer to give credence to such
inanities rather than find out for themselves what they need
to know. The how-to sex books sell millions of copies because they partake of the American dream of success-by-
formula: Ten Easy Ways to a Happy Sex Life—wealth,
health, peace of mind, or what-have-you.

"I'm getting a complex because I don't have multiple
orgasms," said a twenty-five-year-old woman who claims to
have "good" sexual relations with her husband. She said
this in all seriousness, even though it took very little probing to learn she did not really want more of the same kind
of orgasm she always managed to produce, in dutiful re-

sponse to his dutiful manipulations, but a different *kind* of sexual experience altogether ... she longed to spend an entire Sunday afternoon in bed, wallowing in sensation, instead of the after-reading-just-before-going-to-sleep kind of sex, which did not allow her to build enough anticipation or excitement.

The people interpreting the experiments of Masters and Johnson might have made it clearer that the "record" of fifty orgasms per session, achieved by one inspired female, has as little bearing on everyday life as the record set for pole vaulting. Moreover, these orgasms were of the "skimming" variety, like a pebble effect on water, which even Dr. Reuben says are "less satisfying" than the normal kind. Perhaps the study *should* have been called Human Sexual Behavior—Under Laboratory Conditions, Using Subjects With Marked Exhibitionist Tendencies. Most people I know would not be able to function, let alone get off, surrounded by all those people and cameras and instruments.

The confusion has been further compounded by certain hard-core radical feminists. Aside from its political overtones, the great vaginal-clitoral controversy is just plain silly. Mercifully, it no longer rages. Women may have come to accept their own experience as more valid than either Freudian or feminist dogma. Once you've *had* a vaginal orgasm, for instance, it's going to be pretty hard to convince you there's no such thing. Perhaps women have found, as I did, that some orgasms are vaginal and some are clitoral, and sometimes it's hard to tell the difference for it's really terrific when *both* areas are being stimulated at the same time, but none of this has much to do with the *feeling* quality of the orgasm, which determines how satisfying it is going to be.

When I conducted my own minisurvey on the subject of the Big O (to learn why what I read had so little to do with what actually happens in bed), the same conclusion came up over and over: a "good" orgasm is an emotional as well as a physical experience. Both men and women tended to devalue the mere physical release and to imply some other dimension of sexuality. One woman told me she rarely has purely physical orgasms, and when she does she sort of wants to push the man away and not know him afterward. Another young woman of twenty-four says she used to tell men, "I'm not really into it," and they'd reply, "I'll *get* you into it." Sometimes she'd let them. "I'd concentrate on the sensations, come quickly, and immediately lose interest— wish the guy would put on his clothes and go home. I'd feel bad for the guy, but that's how it was."

A number of women declared they had orgasms more easily without too many preliminaries. "I tend to get over-stimulated," explained Heather, the romantic English-woman. Renata found that too much excitement inhibited climax, and so did Rachel. "I love sex," she said, "and half the time I'm not even sure I came or not, I'm so into it."

Another woman told me, "Sometimes I've come easily and it wasn't all that great, neither the sex nor the orgasm. At other times I've been in a state of bliss, turned on to my very toes, without actually coming. I reach a kind of plateau and stay there, and after a while the tension drains away. I'm quite content, but the men are always very concerned. I'm so sick of having to apologize, of saying, 'No, really, it was great!' "

Obviously, not all women experience sex in the same way, and it occurred to me I might be dealing with females who had, in the sexperts' jargon, "sex-negative" attitudes. Then I talked with Zap-prone Lanie. "I've never had any trouble coming," she told me. "I can come with anybody, any time, any place." Something about the way she said it made me ask, How important is it to you? Lanie laughed. "Obviously, not very important, since I can get it off so easily. Don't misunderstand me, I think having an orgasm is very nice. And sometimes it can be sublime—it can transcend you. It happens rarely. When it does, it gets up into your brain."

Lanie's sexuality seems to parallel that of some of the men I talked with. "Just because you ejaculate doesn't mean you really got off," one young man told me. Others said they don't like to come every time they make love. A thirty-six-year-old sculptor, who specializes in erotic art, explained, "I don't like to come that often because it drains you—you lose your interest in sex." He said he enjoys sex enormously and feels no frustration when, after a considerable amount of time, his energy and erection give out.

At least men don't resort to faking it, a practice recommended by quite a few sex books. But a former call girl told me you get more money, these days, if you *don't* fake it—even the Johns are getting wise. A woman Danny once lived with told him after the affair was over that she used to fake it all the time. "It's gotten so sick," he said, "that a woman comes not for her own enjoyment but to gratify the man's ego. Men have co-opted women's orgasms for themselves, so once again, it's the same old story."

This sentiment was echoed by a married woman who, unlike most of the people I talked with, tended to express herself in rather orthodox and cliché feminist terms. "Orgasm is a male success symbol," she said, "a man's idea of achievement. Sure it's an important part of sex, but I think way too much emphasis is being placed on it."

Which may be why Dr. Seymour Fisher, in his six-hundred-page tome called *The Female Orgasm*, found no correlation between orgasmic capacity and either mental health or the degree of subjective satisfaction derived from sex. Nor did he find any correlation between orgasmic capacity and religious attitudes, early training, or any particular technique or time span. He *did* find that middle-class, educated women had more orgasms than working-class women, and so did those women who engaged in sex for its own sake, rather than to achieve status as girlfriends.

The heroine of the film *Made for Each Other* tells her mother she finally had an orgasm with a man she loves. "In my day, there was no such thing," the mother replies, with a mixture of pride and regret. Yet she comes across no crazier or unhappier than her daughter. And James Baldwin pointed out to Norman Mailer, in a radio debate years ago, that where he grew up men and women had orgasms all the time, and still cut each other up with razors on Saturday nights.

If orgasm were really what sex is all about, more of us would settle for masturbation. It is, after all, the surest, quickest, most economical way to get there. Not only are you totally in control, but (as someone in *The Boys in the Band* remarks) you don't have to look your best. But even the sexperts, moralists at the core, condone masturbation only as a means to the end of achieving better sex with a partner. The workout tool frequently recommended for women is the vibrator. One young woman said she had tried it, and not liked it. "It was so . . . well, *plastic*," she explained. Plastic orgasms are all very fine, if you like that kind of thing (although the most recent findings suggest vibrators may damage sensitive tissues).

But training with a vibrator in order to have better sex with people is like practicing the electric guitar in order to become proficient on the harpsichord. (Even the anonymous author of *The Sensuous Woman* warns that the vibrator might "spoil" you.) Lanie summed up the case, putting her finger, as it were, on what was missing in masturbation: "Nothing to touch but your own body."

At one time, sex was something a man did *to* a woman; with the advent of the myth of the Big O, it became something he was supposed to do *for* her. The next step must be the realization that sex is something people do *with* each other. This means we must accept equal responsibility for what happens in bed. We must be prepared to reveal ourselves and tell the truth. In sexual matters, silence, evasions, lies, and deception (in the guise of pleasing) are still the order of the day. So false assumptions go unchallenged and we keep to ourselves the knowledge that the emperor, really and truly, has not a stitch of clothing on.

For, as Masters and Johnson put it, "To *know* is one thing; *to be comfortable* with what one knows is another; to *choose* what is right for oneself is still another."

2
Female Sexual Emancipation Versus the New Impotence

Since women have emerged from their sexual closets, it is becoming more and more intolerable to play the old waiting games; to undergo the agony of longing for that telephone call, or the humiliation of inventing ruses and strategies to get the man to make the first move.

Women's right to sexual satisfaction is something men can relate to and accept; thus they will labor diligently to "give" the woman her orgasm, lest they be considered selfish brutes or, worse, unskillful lovers. But this business of women taking the sexual lead is something else again. It is here that the cichlid effect is triggered most often— that the gap between belief and behavior yawns the widest.

Nearly every one of the men I talked with told me he *liked* the idea of women taking the sexual initiative. They all claimed they longed to be "seduced." But as the conversation progressed, it became apparent that this desire was largely a fantasy. When it came right down to the nitty-gritty, there were considerable problems.

The man who took women home because they expected it said what he likes about having women take the sexual initiative is that it means fewer pressures on him to live up to his traditional masculine role. He went on in this vein for a while until I asked him, point-blank, about his ex-wife, and the other women he'd been seriously involved with.

They tended to play traditional female roles, he admitted. I pointed out that many men feel threatened by women who come on to them, though they might like the idea in theory. On the deeper levels, where sexuality and emotions operate, they find themselves turned off by certain women, often without knowing why.

"That's true," he said. "And they'll come up with some defensive reaction . . . she's really a dyke. She's a ball breaker. You see, liberation is tougher for men. They never talk about 'their inadequacies; they brag about their conquests. The woman of mythology—that lustful thing who can have endless orgasms—is a threat because you figure, How can I satisfy a woman like that? Men love to fantasize about this kind of woman. But if they were to encounter one in real life, they'd run like hell.

"I'm convinced a lot of men who in female terms would be seen as quite eligible turn to pornography not as sublimation or second best or because the real outlets are blocked. These men lead essentially masturbatory lives out of choice, not necessity. Here's this woman on the page, she doesn't give you any argument."

This man's background—New York intellectual-liberal—makes it hard for him to accept the fact that human behavior has a stubborn tendency to fly in the face of logic. He thinks highly of the European custom of young men being initiated by older women and admits he didn't really learn about sex until he ran into a couple of women who taught him. Of course, the older woman is not a potential mate, or an equal—her age puts her at a psychological disadvantage. And once the young man knows, or thinks he knows, what he's doing, he looks for a younger, inexperienced woman whom he can teach what he has learned.

We talked about the fact that men need to feel in charge sexually. Even if they are "liberated" in the sense of the kinds of things they are willing to do, they want to feel they are "giving" the woman her pleasure. As a result, they usually wind up with women who are considerably less high-powered sexually than they are. "The thought that another guy could do just as well is very disturbing," this man explained. "You assume the woman is always making comparisons, and you wonder, am I as good as the last man?"

Danny recalled a woman who once propositioned him at a party. "I felt just like a girl, and I said something like, 'But I don't really know you.' I realized how stupid that sounded, but I really felt it and meant it. She just looked at me in shock and contempt and said, 'Would you like me to find a nice guy for you?' "

I asked him if he'd ever been propositioned and had accepted. Yes, he said, a couple of times. "I knew I was being used as a sexual object, as they say, but I didn't mind, because the girls were nice." However, he didn't see either of the women again. It was just a thing of the moment, he explained.

"I don't want to pursue anymore," said Buddy the bed-hoper, insisting that he'd dearly love to be propositioned. "I will go through the normal procedures of social intercourse, and in the course of it, I'd like a woman to seduce me. Not as a test or anything. I'd like the day to come when women will pursue men as openly and with as much impunity as men have pursued women. When that happens, we will have a very interesting state of equality."

I pointed out that aggressive pursuit on the part of the male, with its implications of hunter and prey, of power enforced and pressure yielded to, has been one of the main stumbling blocks to happy relations between the sexes. When women reverse the roles, the situation is not really changed. Where there is a seducer and a seducee, it always involves a challenge and a risk; a degree of unwillingness, or reluctance, overcome. One or the other puts him/or/herself up for rejection. Why not try to do away with the concept of seduction altogether, of pursuing or being pur-

sued? That might make for a much more interesting state
of equality.

"I would like to know that there is a desire, a sexual
desire, in front," said Buddy. "Otherwise it doesn't matter."

Well, we'd all like to know that. But we can never be
sure, even when we are being actively pursued. One man
told me that when he was growing up the most interesting
thing about sex was that women weren't supposed to do it.
And if they did it with you, it meant they really liked you.
Now, he said, the real meaning of the experience is very
hard to ascertain. You don't know *why* she is doing it.

Still, there is the problem that someone has to make the
first move, Buddy said. You don't just look at each other
across a crowded room and fall into each other's arms.
Despite all the songs, that just doesn't happen very often.
He insisted that it's now the woman's turn to take the
initiative. Even if it means she is sometimes rejected.

Renata also feels very strongly that we must keep on trying, that we cannot give up the struggle to change the
pattern of male-female encounters despite the setbacks,
rejections, and humiliations it might entail. "Our impulse is
not to be positive when we would want to be," she said. "We
can't set it up, make it happen in another time and place.
So we are constantly living in a masochistic situation, waiting to be chosen, and it's a *nightmare*.

"Even if the direct approach isn't successful right away,"
Renata continued, "at least we won't be sitting ducks. After
all, men are being rejected all the time. And *we* are being
rejected all the time, and in a much worse way because we
are not able to aspire, we are not able to express ourselves.
We have to quit being sponges. I find myself meeting someone I like and never being able to see him again because of
what we were talking about before—namely, that men
aren't aggressive anymore, the *macho* thing has shifted;
it's hip not to pursue anymore, because they know the
women are all out there anyhow, and there's this deep
depression operative in men."

I asked Renata if she'd had much success putting her

ideas into practice. Personally, I had found that when I took men up on their professed desire to be seduced, they might go along with the program, but their hearts weren't in it—there was something amiss; no friendly feelings, a chill in the air, a resentment. It's difficult to persevere when you keep being rejected—and not even outright, but in some weird, subtle way you don't know how to deal with.

"You have to be able to take the rejection and not have it throw you back in the closet," Renata insisted. She told me she was now able to do things like send off notes. "I went to a friend's house for dinner and met this man: strange, interesting, just divorced. He tried on my expensive sunglasses. He put them in his pocket and forgot and left. He doesn't have a phone so I wrote a note, asked for the glasses back, and invited him to come for dinner and drinks. He called immediately and is coming over tomorrow."

How did she know he wouldn't have called on his own? I asked. Because she waited over a week, said Renata. And without the excuse of the sunglasses—which is like the old ruse of leaving something behind so you'll have a reason to go back—she wouldn't have written the note. "But two years ago I wouldn't have done *anything*," said Renata. "*Because* I was attracted to him, I wouldn't have asked for the glasses back."

What happens to the woman who comes right out with it, calls or writes, without any excuse? "She's considered a monster," said Renata. "Even if the man takes her up on the invitation, he still thinks she's a weirdo."

Did she mean the man would think the woman was easy, a pushover? "All women are easy now," Renata replied. "No, he'll think there's something wrong with her—she's crazy."

(Note: The gentleman came for drinks and dinner and returned the sunglasses. Period. Renata did not see him again.)

The men I talked to, with few exceptions, strongly resisted the suggestion that their seduction-fantasy-come-true might be a source of more anxiety than pleasure. "Are there really men who don't want to be seduced?" asked Buddy. Of course they want to be seduced, and will agree readily enough to spend the night with the woman who's chosen them. What happens when they get into bed is quite another matter. Not one of the men could recall an instance where, having accepted the sexual advances of a woman, he spent more than a night or two with her. Of course, there was always some *other* reason given why he did not care to see her again.

Some men do understand the difficulty and are struggling with themselves in an effort to overcome their fears. Among them is Gerald, a psychologist and practicing psychotherapist. Though he claims to belong to no particular school, his orientation and vocabulary are mostly *Gestalt,* and he talks a great deal about "getting in touch with your feelings." Gerald is forty-two; an early, conventional marriage which lasted ten years has left him permanently disenchanted with the institution.

Like all the men I talked to, Gerald deplored the fact that men have to be the sexual aggressors. "I've always envied women the privilege of not having to initiate. It was only after my marriage broke up and I ran into a couple of women who had been around that I learned anything. You can't really invent the wheel all the time. You need people who've had their experience and you've had yours and you can learn together."

However, Gerald admitted he's had problems. His psychological training enabled him to be quite specific about the nature of the difficulties and, apparently, to overcome them to some extent.

"My girlfriend and I were making love," he recalled, "and she climbed on top and wanted to take charge. She's quite a strong woman, physically.... Anyway, I went through all sorts of changes and my erection disappeared. I thought, I'm losing control. What does that make me if she fucks *me?* Am I a homosexual? It took a while before I was able to say, Wow, that's great. I *trusted* her, that's important, and in the end I was able to relax and not feel I had to *do* anything. Like, unless I perform, I'm not a man. I remember the feeling of danger. Often, women have climbed on top, but I haven't relinquished control. This time, I just completely let go—didn't even move, just allowed her to do what she wanted."

Of course, a woman who comes on strong sexually, or who asks a man to go to bed with her—or even to come to her place for dinner—is taking her chances. If she's rejected, in one form or another, that's the breaks. Now she knows what men have been up against all these years. But what if the woman doesn't actually take the lead? What if she merely accepts, but does so eagerly, refusing to act coy and honestly admitting she wants what the man wants? Wouldn't this make everybody happy? You might think so. But it seems the specter of the devouring woman is not so easily banished.

Young women, lovely to look at, sexually willing and able, complained to me, in tones of hurt bewilderment, that when they stopped saying no, the men ran away. One young woman, only twenty-three, had observed that all the "free" young men she knew seemed to wind up with women who insisted on the whole traditional structure—marriage, children, security. She guessed they needed these women to help them conform, so they might be "forced" to do what they really didn't like to do—get jobs, settle down, assume responsibility.

For the New Woman is a threat not only in terms of sex. Man has too long relied on woman to be the conservative party, to hold him back and tie him down, so he can strain against the bonds and thus define his freedom. Of course, he resents the constraints. But when they are loosened, he becomes afraid. And impotent.

The New Impotence is *in*—part of radical chic. When *Esquire* magazine, no less, runs a lead article on the impotence boom, one wonders if there's really more of it, or if men are simply admitting it now and dealing with it more

openly. Every man I talked with admitted he had been
impotent at one time or another—in one form or another.
To my surprise, these men readily agreed that premature
ejaculation was one kind of impotence. It's what Danny
meant when he said he got in and out as quickly as possible
when he didn't care about a woman. Others told me they
were able to get an erection but could not sustain it long—
this was perhaps the most frustrating kind of failure, for
themselves and the women, and the men tended to blame
alcohol and/or marijuana for such difficulties. None of the
men I spoke to mentioned women's liberation (perhaps out
of deference to me), but the term "ball breaker" came up
with disconcerting frequency.

Some party-line feminists are all in favor of this development. Who needs a cock? they ask. One New Impotence spokesman, writing in *Ms.* magazine, urged impotents
of the world to unite and come out of their closets. One way
to overcome the stigma, he said, was to stop calling it
impotence. He suggested we call it "erective dysfunction."

However, erective dysfunction is related to impotence, in
the larger sense of powerlessness, in ways that have nothing
to do with the women's movement—or even the sexual
revolution. It has to do with the fact that most men, even
those in positions of power, feel ineffectual—the world has
become too complex for them to act upon it with any degree
of effectiveness. Their feelings of powerlessness and frustration are most easily vented upon women—as they have
always been. Only now, since the woman wants it, hostility
takes the form of denying her sex, rather than forcing it
upon her.

This aspect of the problem was brought out by a thirty-
nine-year-old actor who looks the prototype of the distin-
guished professional man; while he gets lots of acting jobs,
bit parts and so on, fame and fortune have so far eluded
him. "Look, about this impotence business," he said. "There
are many things that will make a man sexually insecure
that aren't necessarily connected with sex. They mostly
have to do with ego. If I go for any length of time without

working, using my talent, or if I go for any length of time without money, then I am weakened. And I can go to bed with a woman and find that I am completely insecure there too.

"The revolution has happened much quicker for women," he explained. "This has to do with the demands of the society we live in. Men are still the main work force of the nation, and a boy still grows up with the threat of war and the draft hanging over him. We have all those veterans— what kind of men for women are these? A lot of them are junkies. A lot don't know how to do anything but fight. There's crime, poverty, corruption, but men are not encouraged to do anything about it, to solve problems."

In the beginning, women aspiring toward sexual emancipation were not angry at men. On the contrary, our hearts went out to the poor creatures who had such heavy burdens placed upon them. We put ourselves in the man's place— small wonder he dropped out on drugs and was impotent some of the time. We would not add to his manifold woes by thwarting him in bed and playing power games with sex. No, we would meet him halfway, and even farther; we would give him the solace of our open hearts and bodies. And of course, we would benefit. After all, sex was beautiful, and love was the answer. Surely, what men wanted was women like ourselves—strong, proud, free . . . *sexy*.

And if it turned out to be not quite so—if somehow the brave new world failed to materialize—you would never have known it from what the men told us. "You're beautiful, baby . . . fantastic . . . the greatest," they'd say, perhaps even sincerely, and were never heard from again. The compliments, freely given, were meant to ease the pain of being kicked upstairs.

So beware, all you Sensuous Women out there! What do you think will happen when you learn to do all those marvelous things, guaranteed to "drive him wild"? You will become this great love goddess, this *femme fatale*, and he will be putty in your hands? Don't you believe it! In all the myths and stories, from Circe to the Hollywood siren, the sexy woman always ends up losing her man—to Penelope, the sweet, spider-patient girl from next door. You may find, as did Germaine Greer, that "many a woman sorrowfully reflects that her more recherché techniques, her more delicate apprehension of her polymorphous partner's need, her very sexual generosity, has entailed her lover's eventual revulsion and estrangement."

Reminiscing about the early days of sexual freedom, Renata said, "I came from Michigan, had never been around any big-city doings. I could have continued schooling or become a copy editor, but instead I shed all my tweedy suits, put on black sweaters, turned on to pot, and went to live in a seedy hotel on Eighth Street. It was real Bohemia, living on oatmeal, total hatred of money . . . a life of fantasy. The reason I was living this way was that I was totally fixated on this guy, sexually. I had met him in the Village, and of course, in those days, when you had an affair you went to live with the guy and made his scene. I never really liked the life of squalor, even though I convinced myself I believed in it. Admitting that I hated the roach-infested little room we lived in would mean I'd have to part with my lover, who was the only person I wanted to share sex with. And sex, which we all confused with love, was then central to my scheme of things."

Not only were the early New Women like Renata dependent on their lovers for the form and setting of their daily lives, but without the emotional matrix these lovers provided, their "liberation," sexual or otherwise, would have floundered and sunk. The "free" girls were also the ones who could be counted upon to be good sports, to take it on the chin with a joke and a grin if the love affair didn't work out, if they were hurt or deceived or abandoned. Free women didn't play games or bargain or cajole—not too much, anyway. That was for the square bitches from the suburbs.

Needless to say, it was the man who was mentor and guide in matters sexual. There was some kind of magic in the act, and things either worked out or they didn't. If they did, you had an affair. If they didn't, you never talked about it, and you remained friends. If you had orgasms, great; if not, nobody worried. You were much too shy to discuss your needs with your partner. Presumably, you were enjoying yourself anyway.

And it was true—in those days, all sexual experience, good, bad, and indifferent, was interesting. Instructive, if nothing else. You would go to bed with men you did not desire, and take your chances on becoming pregnant, just because you liked them and they wanted you. And never for a moment did you feel used or exploited, firmly believing that yours was a privileged way of life.

But, of course, one cannot remain innocent forever. The pattern goes something like this: a man, genus lover, finds a young inexperienced woman with natural talent and proceeds to turn her on ... to guide her in exploring the mysteries of sexual love. What happens then is that, at some point, she catches up and begins to outdistance her guide in boldness, in her eagerness to abandon herself to the murky intoxications of Eros. And suddenly, the man is alarmed. What have I done? he thinks, Pygmalion-style. Where is she *off* to? That's dangerous territory out there! He is afraid; he needs to stick to safer ground, solid, goal-oriented sex, with orgasm as the goal post.

At first he tries to control the woman, to hold her back. But he senses her dissatisfaction, her need to let go. "It is almost always the same with a woman," says Marco Vassi, in his novel, *The Saline Solution*. "We begin together and then she sinks into a swoon of rapture, thinking the depth of her mindlessness was all she ever had to do to please me."

In a woman, aggression is abandon, according to Vassi, and abandon is aggression. At any rate, the man feels he has no choice but to withdraw, leaving the woman high and dry with her now-useless passion. For she cannot simply go on to another partner—it doesn't work that way. It is the love and trust she feels for the man that makes her so ready and eager for abandon.

"Where are we now," asks Ingrid Bengis in *Combat in the Erogenous Zone,*

> having experimented and explored the possibilities? Most of us are stuck ... not knowing what the next step is, aware that we have stumbled upon a complexity we would never have dreamed existed: having increased our expectations, we have also increased our disappointments; having taken the risks, we are feeling the consequences.

At the root of Bengis's man-hating is rage against the men who turn you on and get you hooked on love-sex, then leave you to fend for yourself while they find another woman to do it to. Then the woman must withdraw, purify herself with anger and contempt—practice celibacy or promiscuity, which amount to the same thing. But the craving remains, nagging softly in her belly, till once again need overrides better judgment and the experience of past pain. And though she hopes against hope, she knows it will be the same: unless she holds back and is untrue to herself, she will lose the man. Each time she is forced to cool herself out, realizing that the man who has urged her on is no longer with her, fury against the man seizes her heart. The man senses the fury, which he does not understand, and it increases even further his fear and hesitation. Why, he wonders, is she so intense?

Why indeed? Perhaps the myth of Adam and Eve and the serpent was about sex after all. Perhaps Adam blamed Eve for leading him into heady regions of sensual ecstasy which partook of the divine, when only procreational sex, which was connected with the animal world and the evolutionary scheme, was permitted by the jealous deity. The Greeks, possibly more sensual by nature, allowed in their religion for the Dionysian rites, which were largely the province of priestesses. But the Old Testament Jehovah was an austere god, mistrustful of passion ... and a male supremacist to boot.

3
"The Libido Is a Myth"

Once I was talking to a man and he put his hand on my knee. I ignored it, went on talking, and eventually he took his hand away. A little later, he accidently brushed my face with his hand. "I'm sorry," he said quickly. I laughed. "You had your hand on my knee, but when you touch my face, you apologize?" "Well," he said defensively, "your face is *personal*."

I have thought at length about the kind of attitude that must have inspired such a remark. The fantasy of impersonal sex, a staple of pornography, has always been a part of man's psychic equipment. But rarely until our own day has it been held up as a norm ... let alone as an ideal. But one aspect of the new sexual morality is the notion that you can have sex in a vacuum, without involving any other part of yourself.

In *Psychic Energy: Its Source and Goal*, the noted psychologist M. Esther Harding, a student of C. G. Jung, describes three stages of sexual development. The first and most primitive she calls the autoerotic stage; it is essentially masturbation, with or without a partner. In the second stage, sex becomes more personalized, and desire is aroused by particular people, who trigger in us emotional as well as physical responses. In the third and final stage of development, the motive for sex becomes the desire for a transcendental experience—for ecstasy.

The progression from stage to stage is accomplished through a process Dr. Harding calls "psychification," whereby we transcend the purely physical aspect of our sexual impulses and gain a measure of control over them. (Psychification does not apply only to sex: via this process an impulse as basic as eating has long played an important role in friendship, hospitality, and religious ritual.)

The new sexual ethos of our times has glorified the so-called autoerotic stage, which is essentially indiscriminating —one partner is pretty much the same as another. But ironically, in the process, the sexual revolution has defeated its very purpose of making sex more gratifying, as well as more accessible. Autoeroticism feeds on fantasy, and the masturbatory imagination works best when the psychic and physical distance between the sexes is greatest. The seclusion and veiling of women, elaborate courting rituals, rigid sex roles—all these serve to heighten the sexual tension to the utmost. (In Latin countries, or in the Near East, where segregation of the sexes is the norm, many men seem to walk around in a permanent state of rut.)

When sex becomes too easily available, however, and too public, there is less build-up of sexual tension and, consequently, less excitement. The fact that Harding's auto-erotic sex is not as gratifying in reality as it is in fantasy was brought out in a fascinating study of successful, middle-aged businessmen and their transactions with call girls. Sociologist Martha L. Stein discovered that the success of the call girl profession, in this age of great sexual availability, lies not in the offer of impersonal sex but, on the contrary, in the fact that the call girl listens, reassures, soothes, flatters, entertains, instructs—in short, offers a variey of psychosocial services.

For many women, autoeroticism takes the form of the cave-man fantasy, according to Dr. Harding. "Such a woman feels herself to be . . . an empty vessel that needs to be filled. She longs to be carried away and overcome." The rape fantasy is the female's way of escaping responsibility and relatedness, which are ever fraught with anxiety.

In *The Sex Diaries of Gerard Sorme*, Colin Wilson describes the feeling of freedom and serenity Sorme experiences when an anonymous woman presses against him at an auction. It takes place in the real world but has the quality of a sexual daydream. The same character finds sex a letdown after the pleasure of seduction; knowing he can sleep with wife or mistress anytime he wants to somehow destroys the excitement. And it's excitement he craves, rather than satisfaction: "Only when desire blazes in me can I overcome indifference; desire turns on it like a flame thrower; my body suddenly carries a current of thousands of volts, surging from some main deep in my unconscious."

Such desire may be triggered by seemingly inappropriate catalysts, which are connected to the unconscious by direct wires of suppressed memories. Wilson's hero wonders why, when he has two lovely women eager and waiting for him, does he get such an overwhelming thrill from glimpses of old fat women in their underwear. Such peculiar desire energizes and makes him happy because it represents pure, unconflicted purpose. In the beds of wife or mistress he may find pleasure, even love, but also the gamut of complex emotions and cross-purposes that inhere in all intimate relations.

So eager are we to divorce sex from emotion that we use the word "chemistry" to describe what is, in reality, a psychological and emotional happening. Dr. Harding explains that sexual attraction involves a process whereby we project certain latent aspects of our own nature onto another person. The object of one's desire sets up certain vibrations in the unconscious which produce the illusion of objective attributes. Confronted with the reality of the human being, this illusion cannot be sustained for long, and soon gives way to the familiar what-did-I-ever-see-in-him/her disenchantment.

The person-centered kind of sex may indeed be a higher stage of development, but, as everyone knows, it can be destructive as well as creative. Sex as an expression of a love bond can be sublime . . . and it can be painful, the source of endless conflict, anxiety, and resentment. Sometimes, the love bond can seem too high a price to pay for good sex. Sometimes, also, the emotional involvement gets so sticky that it inhibits rather than enhances the sex. Thus it has become fashionable to discredit the connection between love and sex.

A twenty-eight-year-old editor of a man's magazine, who chafes under what he feels are atavistic restrictions imposed upon him by his wife, told me: "Sex has two functions. One is physical, and the other is social—acceptance, power, the whole bit. But as for all that communion business, I think it's crap, except for the purely physical communion of connecting with a baseball."

"You know, he once told me sex was just like brushing his teeth," said his twenty-six-year-old wife. "I get angry when he talks like that. It hurts me, and it's not really true."

True or not, it is an ideological stance taken by many who have failed to understand that the emotional significance of sex is not confined to the love bond. This "communion business" goes beyond relating to another person . . . it involves getting in touch with a deeper part of yourself. "The desire for ecstasis, though not felt by everyone, bespeaks a widespread and deeply-felt need in human beings," says Esther Harding. While it is true that the lover's attention must be concentrated on the partner, the experience nevertheless is *"not one of union with the beloved* [my italics], but a completely separate and separating absorption in an inner happening of the greatest significance."

The psychological value of the ecstasy experience is a sense of renewal and transformation. It is a kind of psychic

orgasm, and it can recharge us even when there is no con-
comitant physical release—as great artists and religious
mystics have long known. It is popularly believed that sex
relieves tension. It is true that a certain kind of sex does
—sex that partakes of love, of passion, ... of ecstasy. But
the more common autoerotic sex may work much like an
addictive drug. People strung out in this way crave ever
stronger and more exotic doses of the powerful sex drug
—and still get no real satisfaction. In a few days, or a few
hours, they will need another fix. Such people are certainly
not inhibited—but neither are they free, for freedom means
choice, the ability to take it or leave it.

When it becomes the equivalent of playing a game of
tennis or brushing one's teeth, sex no longer has the power
to discharge the tension and frustrations of our daily lives.
There might just possibly be some correlation between the
banalization of sex and the prevalence of violence today. It
is likely that the rapist, the mugger, the murderer also experience their moments of ecstasy. For the experience of
ecstasis is not always benign. It is least dangerous in a
simple sexual context, but the experience always involves
a kind of surrender—a temporary loss of ego and control
which can be extremely threatening. Dr. Harding explains
that in ecstasis, the individual loses his personal self, but
that this is felt to be a gain rather than a loss. "Something
of greater power and authority and dignity than his ego
takes possession of his house," she says. However, many
people do not know how to accept this kind of experience
and integrate it into their lives.

Colin Wilson sees sex as a force that demands a definite
"descent"—a loss of pride and dignity. He further speculates that the value of sex lies in its life-enhancing quality.
"There is no such thing as sex for its own sake," says
Gerald Sorme at one point in Wilson's novel. "The libido is
a myth."

This descent and loss of ego seems to be more of a threat
to men than it is to women (though Dr. Seymour Fisher
notes in his previously mentioned book, *The Female Or-*

gasm, that he found the fear of losing control a major factor in female orgasmic impairment). It may well be one reason men seem so mysteriously reluctant to yield to the ecstasy of passionate, romantic love. It is certainly the reason they get so uncomfortable about "all that mystical shit," as one man put it. But passion is no more and no less mystical than electricity, which we have learned to use, though we still don't know what it *is*. Like electricity, sex can charge you; it can burn you and blow all your fuses . . . or you can plug into a bad connection and fail to produce any juice.

The fact is, everybody gets lonely and everybody gets horny. It doesn't mean we always can or must do something about it. For you can be even lonelier and hornier if you have sex with the wrong person—or perhaps the person might have been right, but the time and the circumstances weren't. We have no patience, no perseverance in matters of sex—it either works right away or it doesn't, and we go on to the next person. And the next. But it's like drinking salt water when you're thirsty.

Still, sometimes it *happens*, people kept saying. Once in a while the magic really works—Sex with the Perfect Stranger . . . Instant Ecstasy. Yes, but only for the first night or two. After that you have to begin to reveal yourself—to relate. Or else you hurriedly retrieve desire, the driving motor, and put it on the lookout for somebody new. Keep bed-hoping, playing the old lottery, for sometimes you win. And besides, what other way *is* there, short of falling in love and all the hassles *that* entails?

There *is* another way. Sexual friendship means just that: a relationship based on friendship which is also sexual in nature. Sounds simple enough, but in practice such a friendship is a rather delicate matter, difficult to sustain. Perhaps, as we become less obsessed with romance, less compulsive about performing, and less fearful of exposing our vulnerabilities, we may be able to combine friendship with sex more successfully. There is a crying need to do so, for even very young people are wearying of the sexual parlor games, of the endless chase. They realize that promiscuity jades you; it dissipates the vital sex energy and reduces the capacity for genuine contact.

"When you go through a long series of one-night stands," said one young man, "you no longer put any *real* value on this aspect of yourself." A young woman of twenty told me kids she knew were "going steady" at sixteen, already fed up with sleeping around, which, she said, was "like singing for your supper. Sometimes you want to be quiet."

Marco Vassi, author of erotic novels, has been called a "mystical pornographer." An avowed bisexual who has experimented widely with offbeat life styles and love styles, Vassi has impeccable credentials as a sexual libertarian; nevertheless, he demolishes the idea of "if they're nice enough to like, they're nice enough to fuck." "Sex is an experience of extraordinary intensity," he said to me in an interview, "a force you have to handle with kid gloves. People want to think it's like something horses do in a field. . . .

"No, it's not like that for human beings. Now if *I* were running things, you'd have to go through a five-year initiation before you were allowed to have sex. And then, once you entered the palace, so to speak, there'd be different tests and degrees; if you were an apprentice or a journeyman, you would not fuck with a master." Vassi was not just talking about technique. He believes that erotic explorations must be conducted in a spirit of reverence.

That sex and religion are polar manifestations of the same force was acknowledged by Wilhelm Reich, as well as by Freud and Jung, though the latter two were careful to couch the matter in scientific terms. But mystics of every faith, throughout the ages and in all parts of the world, have had no such compunctions, and have persisted in using the image and symbol of sexual union to describe their experience of religious ecstacy. The prophets and priests and holy texts of every creed have sought, with varying degrees of subtleness and success, to reconcile sex and religion.

Lingam worship, temple prostitutes, bacchanalian orgies, tantric sex, the "holy" sacrament of marriage, the "vows" of chastity—all were means of putting sex in the service of the deity. But no method of regulating the sex drive has ever had more than partial and relative success—for a certain time, in a certain place, with certain people.

According to *The Tibetan Book of the Dead*, the departed soul wanders in limbo for forty-nine days; during this time, it begins to fall prey to sexual fantasies. It becomes attracted by visions of mating couples, is eventually caught by a womb and reborn into the world. This metaphor suggests that it is our unresolved, unassimilated sexual dreams that continue to trap us in the existential cycle—birth, the battle of the sexes, death. It offers a clue as to why the Judaeo-Christian concept of willful control and suppression has been so notoriously unsuccessful. The only way out of the cycle is by a kind of spiritual leap or breakthrough, which involves a descent into those reaches of the unconscious where the life force disguised as sex, manifestations of the occult, and the genuine intuitions of reality all reside. The trip through dark regions must be made—the repressed fantasies brought into the open and acted out, if necessary—by all who want to save their souls.

This is the true significance of the often ill-advised and destructive experiments with mind-expanding drugs, as well as the so-called sexual revolution. It is not really a matter of kicks. The symbolic descent into hell—fantasy enactment, madness, ecstasis—can be extremely dangerous. But without it, no true regeneration is possible; at a certain point in the development of the individual, the journey becomes necessary, and fear and doubt must be overcome (it was doubt that made Orpheus lose Euridice), though caution and self-discipline are indispensable.

In times of social decadence and dissolution, people turn to sex, out of an intuition that here is something real—something tangible to cling to while everything else fades and falls apart. We long for the abandonment, the release from self that sex can bring, and the more we indulge our lusts, the stronger becomes this longing. Over and over, we try to find the magic land, for haven't we been told the way lies through the hay? Once upon a time, sex and love and spirit were one, and we were not split apart . . . or is this only the collective dream of the race?

The more we talk and write about sex—the more we depict its mechanics in hard-core, technicolor close-ups —the more its essence seems to elude us. Technique and experience don't really help much. For when we *think* we know, we are no longer open—we don't bring to the experience what a famous Zen master has called "beginner's mind." It doesn't mean innocence, for the novice may have a host of preconceptions of how sex "ought" to be. And one may realize, after much trial and error, that it is not possible to program our sexual experience—at least not without losing a great deal.

I do not mean to suggest that sex can or must partake of ecstasis all the time, only that we ignore this facet of it at our peril. Nor do I mean to imply that the spirit of reverence is synonymous with solemnity. All the different moods and modes of sex have their time and place and value: playful sex, low-key and relaxed; tender sex, gentle and affectionate; theatrical sex, stylized and elegant; procreative sex, intense and serious; Rabelaisian sex, bawdy and wild—all these and many more can bring joy and release and renewal. Nor is there anything the matter with masturbation. The autoerotic mode persists to a large extent, and fills a special need even for those able to experience sex at more complex levels.

Provided there is a basic respect for the forces one is dealing with, and that they are not a substitute for real participation, play and art can greatly enhance sexual enjoyment. It is only when we are fearful, or bored, or miserly, or cruel, or calculating—when we use sex to show off, gain power, bargain, or humiliate—that no renewal is possible. Instead, we end up feeling dissipated—disappointed and frustrated. For when we engage in sex without the fuel of desire, we are doing something very peculiar, and ultimately damaging, to that intricate mechanism, the sex drive.

Fortunately, this mechanism has always been extremely resilient. The current disenchantment with the sexual revolution is just another example of the triumph of the sex drive, which has survived countless attempts to tame, suppress and subvert it. I don't believe it was ever in serious danger of succumbing to the onslaughts of the second half of the twentieth century.

Already, the change in the air is noticeable—the tide of opinion is unmistakably turning. More and more people are re-evaluating their thinking and behavior with regard to sex. The massive dropping out, the avowed impotence, the increase of voluntary celibacy among those with other options—all might just be people's ways of stepping back for a bit to gain a clearer perspective on what's really going on.

Perhaps "sex" is a term both too limited and too all-embracing. Colin Wilson may be nearer the mark when he calls it the Life Force. "Sex is the nearest thing to magic . . . to the supernatural, that human beings ever experience," he writes in *The Sex Diaries of Gerard Sorme*. "No study is so profitable to the philosopher. In the sex force he can watch the purpose of the universe in action."

bonding

1
Pair Formation

There is a popular belief that love-and-marriage have become uncoupled in contemporary America. The figures on the divorce rate, which we've all heard *ad nauseam*, tell us that one out of every three—and in some states, like California, one out of every two—marriages ends in divorce. How, then, do we account for those other statistics—the ones on *marriage*? Two out of three Americans of marriageable age *are* married, after all. More ceremonies are being performed now than at any other time since the 1945–1946 postwar boom, and the number of marriages continues to rise each year. People are marrying younger and younger, and most of the folks who are part of the divorce statistics one year become part of the marriage statistics a few years later, when they are wed again.

And these are only the figures on *legal* marriage. If we take into consideration the growing number of extralegal unions, both hetero- and homosexual, it seems safe to assume that almost all adults will be, at some time in their lives, involved in some kind of marriage-like arrangement.

One of the most fascinating aspects of this data is that the nuclear family is being supplanted, more and more, by the "subatomic" family—a household containing two adults only.

The two-person ménage now constitutes thirty-five percent of the total number of American families. When you add the unrecorded number of people shacking up—gay and straight, young and *old* (there is a growing trend among retired widows and widowers who cannot afford to lose the woman's pension or Social Security to cohabit without benefit of clergy or law)—you might justifiably conclude that pair formation seems to be the preferred form of human bonding in our time.

But even if the traditional marriage-as-an-institution is indeed moribund, it could go on dying by inches for an extraordinarily long time—as long as we continue the social and economic life-support systems we now lavish upon it. Thus, all the lamenting and hand-wringing seem a little beside the point. Sociologist Ira L. Reiss points out, in the anthology *Marriage: For and Against*, that "if we change marriage to a ceremony with a rock band, or hold that sharing a room signifies marriage, we are not eliminating marriage, only changing its form."

Although marriage cannot be the same for us as it was for our grandparents, we still enter into it hoping the union will be permanent. Nevertheless, the knowledge that divorce is a possibility must color the marital bond in more or less subtle ways. In fact, there is reason to believe that divorce actually *supports* marriage, by providing an escape valve, in the same way that adultery and prostitution have served to support it.

To be sure, we are no longer quite so innocent. Nevertheless, the dream lives! Although we know more about the enormous possibility of failure, paradoxically that only seems to make the goal more enticing than ever. What's more, we have become more and more demanding in what we want and expect from marriage. Deprecating the importance of the formalities and legalities, we approach love-

and-marriage today in the spirit of the diehard gambler: it's all or nothing at all, and if at first you don't succeed, try for the jackpot next time.

And indeed, the jackpot is quite a boodle. It means that love will grow, and *last*—if not forever, at least for a considerable time. It means all your sexual, emotional, and spiritual needs will be fulfilled by just one other person, so that you will need no one else and can forgo all other intimate relations. You will share everything, all your joys and sorrows, all your interests; you will always tell each other the whole truth and nothing but the truth (except for the "little white lies" to save each other's feelings). You will have complete trust in each other (except when someone else is paying too much attention to your spouse, in which case you will exhibit jealousy as proof of your great love). You will be together every moment you possibly can, and will always want to do the same things and go to the same places at the same time.

"I am you and you are me and we are one," is how it's put. "I'm a romantic," people say defiantly and somewhat proudly, meaning: "I'm an idealist and I'm looking for perfection, not like the rest of you cynics." (It is interesting to observe those who *have* achieved this dream of oneness—and lost their identities along the way. They're the couples who end up looking like each other.)

In the way the lawyers, psychologists, and other professionals regard the business of marriage and divorce, there is a definite conflict of values. On the one hand, they uphold the traditional view that marriage is sacrosanct (which implies that a loveless marriage is morally superior to an illegal love bond), and on the other hand, they support the romantic idea that adultery and alienation of affection constitute the most valid (and often the only acceptable) grounds for divorce.

This attempt to have it both ways is typical of the point of view of both the popular experts and the social scientists who write about marriage. The psychologist Israel Charny declares that marriage is inherently a "disturbingly difficult state," and that virtually all marriages are deeply disturbed. On the positive side, however, he writes, in *Marital Love and Hate*:

> There's a real value to contracts. They offer a framework of security against rashly impulsive blowing up of relationships. Commitment to marriage ... offers a sense of security [there's that word again!] and meaning to one's self and one's family, especially if the going gets rough, as it always does.

Well, I don't know. Is a difficult and disturbing marriage more secure than a long-standing extralegal bond? People I know who have lived together for a time are very reluctant to break up. Whether they are legally married or not, they tend to hang in there as long as they can.

Margaret Mead sees the nuclear family as obsolete, but she feels marriage can and should be saved and has made a famous proposal for marriage in two stages. The first phase would be individual, with two people deciding to live together; this would be a lightweight marriage, easily dissolved. The second stage, the parental marriage, to be entered upon with the advent of the first child, would be just like the marriage we have now. How this arrangement, which for all intents and purposes already exists, unofficially, is supposed to do away with the nefarious nuclear family is something I quite fail to see.

Nena and George O'Neill, of *Open Marriage* fame, start out by telling it straight:

> Most of the unrealistic expectations surrounding marriage are cast in the form of promises of *security* [my italics].... Couples depend on marriage to *give* them a purpose and meaning in life, to give them love and affection, social acceptance, status. Such couples will seek the cause of their troubles anywhere but in their own distorted view of what marriage *should* be....
> Many people frantically scrounge around for any partner who will have them and rush into

marriage just to acquire that badge of identification—Us—A Couple.

The O'Neills go on to ask, rhetorically, "Can we find virtues in marriage other than that most alternatives are chancier and at least marriage provides the assurance of the known?" Their answer, apparently, is yes. And here's the revolutionary reason why: "Aside from tradition and social pressure, man has an innate need for structure and form—especially in our complex, chaotic society." According to the O'Neills, "Institutions are . . . our way of formalizing some of the structures underlying human behavior."

Like other marriage experts, the O'Neills only point up the universal ambivalence with respect to this subject. A man I know who has been married five times and divorced four explained that he couldn't live *with* marriage and he couldn't live without it. When my first husband told me he was getting married for the third time, I said to him, not unkindly, "You got a lot of heart." He laughed, but admitted he was "marriage-prone"—that he would probably be married to someone or other the rest of his life.

What, then, in this day and age, does legal marriage have to offer people who are not motivated by religion or social pressure? You'd think people who have been through the psychological and financial horrors of divorce would be extremely reluctant to risk going through all the ceremony and paper-signing again. Such is not the case, however, and second marriages (which have been called the triumph of hope over experience) tend to be the rule. Since none of the professionals have anything to say in favor of legality that doesn't sound lame and/or trite, I asked a number of my acquaintances, who have no axes to grind and a larger stake in understanding what's going on than in preserving an institution, why they got married.

The reasons given were largely practical—sometimes a question of cold cash. One woman married her second husband, a stockbroker, on January 1, "so he could claim me as a deduction for the whole year." (They had been living together for nearly that long.) Others cited the difficulty of obtaining credit, of renting and, especially, buying a house. (It *can* be done—I know a couple who have lived together for thirteen years and bought a house in their own separate names—but it is difficult, and often embarrassing.)

Let us suppose you want to take out life insurance for the person you are living with. You will find, first of all, that there is no proper designation for that person. "Lover" is too heavy and romantic; "friend" too casual and unspecific. The common journalistic euphemism "companion" is also too ambiguous. What else? Old Man? Boyfriend? Mistress? You see the problem. Although in many circles this type of union is the rule rather than the exception, it still has no name, let alone any kind of status.

The first time I got married it was for the money we were going to get from our relatives. Ostensibly, we didn't believe in marriage (this turned out to be not quite true, since we both wound up marrying again). My first husband came from a large Jewish family where the custom (of recent origin and very American) is to give checks as wedding presents. We knew we stood to receive about three thousand dollars, a vast sum of money, in those days, for a couple just starting out in life. (Since my parents spent at least that amount for the wedding, the bribe all in all came to better than $6,000.)

Also, we thought getting married would get our families off our backs and make them happy. Well, it may have made them happy, for a while (until they started to fret about the absence of babies), but it certainly didn't get them off our backs—quite the contrary. Once you have done the legal thing, the in-laws usually assume certain rights: to make demands on your time, to visit and be visited, to offer advice, to pressure for further conformity, and in general to interfere with your life. Looking at the situation more positively, marriage can provide the extended family many of us miss. But it's not the same as getting your family off your back, and it definitely runs counter to the American credo that marriage is a private and personal matter between two people.

One woman explained: "I was so worn out from the pressure of my family. They didn't care about my accomplishments, the books I had written. All my mother did was grieve over me, the failure in life." She has known she was a lesbian since she was ten, had been having lesbian affairs since she was twenty, but she got married at the age of thirty to the first man who asked her. Within the space of three years, she had two children and got divorced. But she had paid her dues to society and "normalcy" once and for all.

Aside from money and parental pressures, there is the matter of social acceptance and status. For many people, being married is the basic irreducible minimum for success in life. Having the right kind of wife is a must for the politician, or the corporation man looking to move up the ladder (though this trend is on the wane as more and more frustrated wives refuse to play the game, taking time and energy away from the man's work with their complaints and demands). Most of the time, however, it is the woman who gains status by marrying. In our couple-oriented society, the single woman over forty is an object of pity and contempt. The social value of a bachelor, of any age, is infinitely higher than that of an unmarried woman, however attractive and accomplished. Still, a man not married by the age of thirty-five is suspected of being a homosexual.

Thus, for a large number of people, the safety and security lie not in their relations with their partners but in the state of being married itself. Marriage is for those who find contentment within habit and tradition, and are not inclined to quarrel with their circumstances.

The ordinary, who constitute the majority in any culture, want to be just like their neighbors. They will consider divorce, and even swinging, if the Joneses and the Smiths down the block are doing it. They like the familiarity and comfort of being boxed in, the safety of having definite boundaries.

"The formality of marriage helps you to get to know someone seriously," said one young woman. Sometimes, though, the formality of marriage means you never have to get to know the person at all, since the roles are so clearly defined. Though rigid role behavior is cited as a major cause of marital misery, there can also be great comfort in it. The very anarchy of the modern world can make a role seem a haven. Paul Goodman, author of *Growing Up Absurd*, spoke of the uncertainties facing young men who are offered no goals worth striving for and pointed out that men often envy women for having the assured destiny of becoming wives and mothers.

Is the nurturing of children, then, the main reason for preserving the legality of marriage? Strangely enough, though many of the people I talked with got married when the woman became pregnant, the fact of her pregnancy was not often given as the reason for signing the document. If the word "bastard" makes you wince, as it should, it only goes to show that the original meaning hardly applies anymore; even the term "illegitimate" is beginning to sound baroque. Furthermore, it is of doubtful legal value, for in many states a man can declare himself the legal father on a birth certificate and give the child his name even if he is not legally married to the mother. The same holds true of wills, and other documents relating to inheritance.

All the same, most women still find it difficult to accept the idea of having children "out of wedlock" (another baroque phrase), for psychological reasons much more than economic or legal ones. The old strictures and taboos are still very powerful and continue to exercise a strong hold over us. Many couples quietly get married when a child is expected, as a kind of gesture—a propitiatory offering to the gods of respectability, in the hope that this will bring good fortune to their offspring.

Does a legal contract, then, offer no realistic protection to a child? What about child support, you may ask? Well, what about it? What about the absurdity, not to say the ethical questionability of marrying so that the man will be obliged to pay child support upon divorce? If a man loves his children and has a sense of responsibility, he will look after them with or without the signed paper; and if he doesn't, that same piece of paper will not prevent him from disappearing into the woodwork, as untold numbers of husband-and-fathers are doing every day.

If a woman wants marriage to "protect" her children, it means she assumes that divorce is likely and that her husband will have to be coerced to do his duty, which gives further credence to the contention that divorce is one of the main socioeconomic supports for the institution of marriage. For if the marriage laws favor the man, as the feminists rightly contend, the divorce laws favor the woman: she need never pay alimony or child support, even if she is financially able and has left her husband and children. But *she* is entitled to child support at the least, even if it is true that she may have difficulties *collecting* these monies from her former husband.

It is divorce, also, which makes possible the contemporary form of marriage which has been given the accurate, if uninspiring, name: serial monogamy. What it means is that you marry one person, and after a period of time you divorce and marry another. Presumably you are faithful and exclusively committed to each of these partners in turn. What serial monogamy does is permit the continuation not only of legal marriage but of *romantic* marriage, based on love and compatibility.

We can accept serial monogamy more easily if we see it as an interim form, offering a compromise between conflicting imperatives: the need for a union based on love and common interests on the one hand, and the need for the structure, status, and security of legality on the other.

"The only people ... for whom the old-fashioned marriage seems to hold a real mystique are homosexuals, who for the first time are able to find clergymen willing to marry partners of the same sex," say the O'Neills. But I would disagree with them on this point: the old-fashioned marriage still seems to hold a real mystique for all sorts of people, including the young, the hip, and the unconventional. How else explain the fact that so many people who have lived together for years and years (overcoming social, financial, and parental pressures) at a certain point decide to go through the legal ceremony after all?

I'm not talking about the people who marry when the woman becomes pregnant. Rather, what seems to happen is that the union reaches a certain stage—you come to a turning point, and then it seems that you must make a choice . . . either to dissolve the bond or to solidify it. Some kind of concrete change seems called for, and what could be more concrete than marriage?

Say you have been living together for four years, and things have gotten a bit stale, a little boring; the thrill is gone and the sex is not quite what you'd like it to be. Say you started out living together in a tentative way, and the whole thing still seems kind of up in the air—despite the fact that you are locked into each other in a thousand small and large ways. Considering the alternatives, you realize you do not want to split up—you cannot even endure to contemplate the emotional wrenching that would involve. So you reason that your dissatisfactions stem from the fact that you are not committed *enough*, that you still think there might be a way out.

For some people, it works—at least for the time being. It means: O.K., this is it! I'm not shopping around any more. "The commitment takes a lot of pressure off," one young man explained. "It frees you to go about the business of living." But for other couples it's like pouring more money into a bad investment.

"When you marry to resolve a crisis, you are basically appealing to magic," says psychologist Carl Rogers in *Becoming Partners: Marriage and Its Alternatives*. "Marriage of itself has some kind of mystical, magical powers to resolve things, to work a miracle."

There is a great lack of ritual and ceremony in our lives, Dr. Rogers notes. Many of us miss these rituals, whether we know it or not, for they have played an important psychological part in human life for millennia, especially in the form of the so-called rites of passage, which mark off the great, distinctive changes we undergo at certain points in our lives.

Living together is becoming, more and more, a form of courtship, often prolonged, as many engagements were in the past. Sometimes even a broken first marriage, entered upon when the participants were very young, can be seen as similar to the broken engagement of yesteryear. For, as we all know, though people are getting married all the time, hardly anybody gets engaged anymore.

When my second husband asked me to marry him, we'd been living together for two years (one of the magic numbers). Since, unlike him, I had already been married and divorced, I was hesitant. "But we're married already," said I. "We have a joint checking account. How married can you get?"

"Well," he said, "it's like putting a frame around the picture." (When I told this story to an artist friend, he pointed out that many paintings today no longer require frames.) What it came down to, then, was: "You mean you *won't* marry me?" How could I not, if that's what he wanted and the symbolism was important to him? And for a time, it *did* seem to lend an added dimension to the bond, for neither of us knew how to forge a deeper commitment without the contract. This second marriage lasted five years. Counting the two years of cohabitation, it came to seven years altogether (another magic number). Neither of us was going to hold to a commitment we no longer wanted just because we had made it legal.

"There was this young woman I lived with all through college," recalled one young man, who admitted he'd been "lucky." "When I graduated, we were afraid to split up; there we were, glued together, and we still loved each other, so we said, 'Let's get married.' And this decision is typical of many people who get married because they can't *not* get married. Then we started to make it real, sent out invitations and so forth, and one day she woke up in tears and said, 'I know we're not doing the right thing.' And without even thinking, I said, 'I'll leave on Monday.' Because I *knew* she was right. There was a great sense of relief, and at the same time, it was *tragic*—we cried and we made love, for three days. But it was the end—we'd gone as far with the relationship as we could."

When people who have lived together get married, it *does* change things—sometimes for the better, sometimes for the worse. When you resort to magic, you are taking your chances, for you don't know whether the magic will be black or white. Getting married to resolve a crisis is like fighting fire with fire, for the signing and the ceremony constitute a crisis all their own. We've all heard the stories. The couple lived together happily for ten years, then they got married. Within a year, they were divorced. While their sex life was fine before, afterward the husband became impotent. Et cetera and so forth.

You can be as blasé about marriage as you like—after all, what difference can a piece of paper make? Then, when you actually get married, you find you have all these ideas stewing around just below the surface. Marriage itself begins to exert a strange kind of force over you, whether or not you attach much importance to it consciously.

Take this classic example: A young couple—let's call them John and Mary—had been living together for three years. She was becoming irritable and bitchy—for no reason either of them could name—and they were quarreling more and more often. One night after a party, they were having a particularly nasty fight and John told Mary to get out. "I don't want to," she retorted. "I live here and I'm going to stay."

"Then let's get married," said battle-weary John, who had finally understood why Mary was being so difficult. So they were married. And lived happily ever after? Not a chance! "When we were living together, we were sort of equal partners in making the living, and if we were broke, nobody really took the blame," John explained. "When we were married, it became *my* fault if there was no money . . . I was the bum who wasn't out looking for work."

John never claims it was his wife who put the onus on him. In part, it was pressure from the in-laws, and for the rest, it was the way he came to feel about *himself*. He had internalized society's values more than he realized.

By and large, it is still the woman who pressures for marriage, despite the fact that women fare worse than men in the married state, psychologically, physically, and financially. Authors of divergent ideologies, including Jessie Bernard, Phyllis Chesler, and George Gilder, all cite statistics which indicate the married woman's bodily and mental health ranks well below that of married men and single women (only single men seem to be worse off). But when facts and myth collide, we know which will be the winner. The woman, who has been relentlessly conditioned toward seeking acceptance and respectability, tends to believe that the magic of marriage will allow her to lie back and relax in the security of wifehood. If so, she may be in for some nasty shocks—from either her husband's behavior or her own, for it may turn out that she herself is suddenly, and unaccountably, in deep psychological trouble.

"When I got married, I suddenly felt my life was over," explained Mary, who was the one who had pushed for marriage. "It was the end. I had nothing to do. I thought I might as well lie down and die. I had ceased to be a person. Also, I thought, when you get married, you don't have to be in love anymore. I wouldn't have to be bothered with John and could go about my merry business."

This rather odd idea, that marriage might be a relief and an escape from the emotional turmoil of being in love, was also expressed by Lanie. "My mother convinced me that if I let my life keep on drifting, I would end up alone and lonely. So I thought, I would have security, I would be a married lady, and my husband was so blah and not there that he would not interfere in any way with who I was. It was a lot of bullshit, of course, but I could hang in there at the beginning because he did not disturb me. My head was dead, not functioning in any way, for about five years."

Most of the people I talked with, including the married, had considerable misgivings about the state of matrimony.

But almost all of them believed that living together was fine—in fact, quite a few of them felt it was "the answer." After all, why must the government get involved in your love life? If you have a need for ritual and crave a symbolic marriage, why not have a party, invite all your friends, and maybe even get one of the new unconventional ministers to perform an unofficial ceremony (those from the Universalist Church tend to be amenable to this sort of thing). The men, especially, were concerned about the disastrous financial aspects of divorce. Why set yourself up for that old Mexican curse, which goes: "May your life be filled with lawyers."

These people have accepted the fact that the pair-bonds we form are not likely to last the rest of our lives.

"The illusion of forever is something that can never be replaced," said the woman who claimed she was a "builder" of relationships. Now nearing fifty, she was married for ten years and has a grown son; she was also involved in a liaison with a married man (whose Catholic wife refused to grant him a divorce) for fifteen years and has another child by him. Despite having "erected a mighty structure," as she put it, this affair has also come to an end, leaving her distraught and on the brink of nervous collapse.

"If the impulse of forever is gone, everything is lighter, nothing has the weight," she explained. "It's like living in a hotel instead of a house."

I pointed out that in many places people buy houses, and even build them, only to sell them again two years later. (The analogy to serial monogamy is obvious, except that the house sellers, unlike the divorcers, often stand to benefit financially.) Although, from my own point of view, the weight of "forever" can be extremely oppressive, this woman persists in believing that it is constructive. "The idea, the commitment, the promise, the expectation of forever—*that's* what marriage is. It isn't the paper or the property arrangement. What makes marriage important is this very heavy thing . . . forever! Everyone knows you can get a divorce. You never get married thinking you can always get a divorce."

Interestingly enough, the people who cannot seem to form any real affectional bonds have the same feelings this woman does. "I cannot take the insecurity of not knowing how long something is going to last," said a man of twenty-seven. "Why get involved when the thing could be over just like that?"

For just as you don't get married thinking you can always get divorced, you don't even start *living* together—buying belongings and building your nest—thinking it's going to end someday. "Permanence is part of the dance," is how one man put it. Part of the dance of courtship and romance is the belief that we can lick the odds—this time it's "the real thing," and that means it's going to last.

If I have dwelt at some length on the subject of marriage, I did not mean to suggest that cohabitation is indeed "the answer," or that the differences outweigh the similarities. People who congratulate themselves on having escaped the legal trap do not necessarily escape the psychological consequences of marriage. For when we form a pair bond—meaning we share sex, affection, and domicile with another person, whether of the same or the opposite sex—we tend to relate the arrangement to the only model we know: the examples and experiences we've been exposed to are those of marriage—in particular, the marriage of our parents. The pull is always toward following a familiar pattern, and, since we usually follow the path of least resistance (which generally turns out to be the toughest), we may well wind up living by the hidden clauses of the contract we never signed.

These clauses are insidious, not only because they are hidden but also because they involve the deepest emotional layers of our beings. Take the matter of jealousy and possessiveness (the former term is most often applied to men, the latter almost exclusively to women; the man's possessiveness is considered legitimate and thus taken for granted). We are well aware that jealousy and possessiveness are no-noes—signs of immaturity and insecurity that erode love. The psychologists are all down on these emotions, as are the commune-oriented young. There is no arguing with the wisdom or good will of those who feel we must forgo jealousy and possessiveness. But tradition and myth tell us otherwise. "You belong to me," says the popular song, and though our mind disapproves, a thrill of yearning courses through our loins, secret regret for the times when passion flared in the breast and the heart beat wildly... "You're mine alone"... "I'll never leave you"... "forevermore"... "my very own."

Most of us would laugh, or cringe with embarrassment, if anyone we knew ever uttered such drivel, yet these phrases come up again and again in the songs we hear on the radio and the jukebox. We listen to them with another part of ourselves, where dream and desire hold sway. The words imprint themselves on our nerves and our viscera (it is the gut, rather than the heart, which is the seat of romantic passion), even when the blatantly sexual beat and the rude sounds from the electric guitar serve to lend the words an ironic, and even cynical, undertone. While we don't really believe in the meaning of the words, we do believe in the *emotions* which generate them.

All you need for a beautiful, free, open marriage, say the O'Neills, is to give up on jealousy and possessiveness, which have, in reality, nothing to do with love. Of course they don't. But jealousy has been so closely linked to coupling that it will take more than a generation or two of enlightened psychology to slay the ancient dragon.

Many anthropologists agree that possessive sex relations run at least as deep as territorial aggression. This does not mean, of course, that what has been true in the past must remain the same in the future. Not long ago, when jealousy and possessiveness were tacitly sanctioned and accepted by society, one could suffer the pangs of jealousy without disgrace, sure of the sympathy of others. But now, the feeling is something to be ashamed of, even though it still gnaws at our innards. We strive mightily to rise above such atavistic emotions, and if we fail we do our best to hide the fact.

Instead of making a scene... having an attack of migraine or menstrual cramps and demanding to be taken home at once, as our old-fashioned girl would, the New Woman swallows the sick feeling, grins and bears it, maybe even starts flirting a little herself—anything rather than put a damper on the animated exchange between her man and that stunning redhead. Guess which woman will hold on to her man longest. The possessive one who drives him crazy. What can he do, she *needs* him so. He may pity her, he may be contemptuous of her dependency, her insecurity, and treat her with disdain. But he's *sure* of her; he understands her games, and that constitutes *his* security.

Just as men prefer to marry women who are less high-powered sexually, they also tend to wind up with women who are less "free" —that is, inclined to be possessive and to insist on sexual exclusivity. Walter and Irma are a good example of this kind of union. He is thirty-one, and has been active in the underground press; she is twenty-nine. Both came originally from the same small Midwestern town and have known each other since high school. They've been married for five years. Though they had agreed to be interviewed together, they kept making excuses and arranging postponements ... they were afraid, as Walter put it, of opening a can of worms.

"I hope I fight the idea of marriage till the day I die," said Walter, "even if it gives me an ulcer. Because I believe giving into it is death." I asked him how he defined marriage, then. "Irma and I share everything," he said, "and we take responsibility for each other." That didn't sound so terrible to me, and I wondered what the problem was. "Fundamentally, we have different philosophies," Walter replied. "We like each other an awful lot. But I believe in maximum freedom for people. And Irma ... well, she's kind of possessive. Definitely possessive." I asked if he was not at all possessive of her. "I'm not as possessive as she is," he said, "though I've gotten a little spiteful lately, which I'm not very happy about. You see, we never come to grips with the situation. What we do every day is live out the unexpressed anxieties of two people who want to be free."

At this point, Irma asked Walter why, if he despised marriage so much, was he still with her. I tried to put the matter more diplomatically: surely there were advantages and satisfactions that outweighed the frustrations? "I don't think Walter will give you a list of satisfactions," said Irma.

"No," said Walter, "I won't give you a list of satisfactions. I will just say that the other way is too dangerous and unworkable. The free-floating life is difficult because it means taking a lot of chances with a lot of people, and you get burned a lot. People are not always ready to handle their own freedoms.

"At one time before Irma and I got married I was making it with five women," he continued. "They all knew each other—things were really nice. I was relating to each of the women in the deepest possible way, it seemed to me. I enjoyed the company of the different women for different reasons, and things were always happening, things were always interesting. I didn't make any demands—I saw them when it was convenient for both of us. Well, within five months, everything fell apart. They went back to their boyfriends, they went back to their husbands—they went back to lives I couldn't understand. I was left out in the cold, wondering what had happened. I'm not perfect, but I wasn't doing anything *that* wrong."

You weren't giving them what they needed, said I. "That's right," said Walter, "and there was no way I could. And after that was when Irma and I finally got married. Because Irma was the one person I could—"

"Make demands on," interrupted Irma, who had been one of the five women, and had let him go along with the others. "People need—at least *I* need—to be needed. It's important that a person who cares for me make some kind of demands on me."

"Given an ideal society," said Walter, "one person would move very fluidly to another. Since most people are not capable of this, they find a particular person to anchor with. Even if that person isn't active in their life at the moment, in their *heads* there's this person they trust most of all. I feel that whatever is between Irma and me is going to be there whether we live together forever, or for another year, or two weeks. Because I've known her for a long time.

"I knew this free-floating girl who used to hold it against me that Irma was my particular anchor, and she used to try to make me feel guilty about it. But this girl had *her* anchor. I wouldn't ask her to give up her anchor—she could go back in the middle of the night. I think it can work—find one person to use as an operating base for your life; take the most nourishment from this person, and take from other people a little bit here and a little bit there."

An anchor, of course, offers no *real* security. Any strong current, or a change in the tides, can loosen the anchor and send you adrift again. At most, anchoring offers a respite...a temporary refuge in a storm-tossed world. But that is already quite a lot. As Walter pointed out, you can get very weary and battered out there, in the open sea. What anchoring involves, however, is commitment—taking responsibility for each other—for without this there can be no trust.

The way Walter defines the anchoring ideal, we have our own lives and retain our freedom, but we're very special to each other and can count on one another when the chips are down...call each other at three in the morning and say, Help!, or whatever. But anchoring rarely happens without the locking in; somehow, that important connection does not take place without the exclusivity, without the promises and the demands, and you drift apart. You can't float free and be anchored at the same time. Walter tried to have it both ways, with his five women, and he wound up with nothing—until he made a firm commitment to one of them.

This is the basic dilemma: to find some acceptable compromise between the security of a stable union, and the need for freedom of movement. Men are afraid to commit themselves for fear of entrapment; women dread the emotional slavery. And the fears are justified. But not having an anchor—someone special to care for who cares about you —can be soul-destroying and dehumanizing too.

In a Schopenhauer parable, two porcupines move together for warmth on a cold day. Soon they hurt each other with their quills and move apart, only to find themselves freezing again. They move back and forth, freezing and hurting, until they find the optimum distance where they can huddle for warmth and yet not pain each other too much.

"You see," said Walter, "the unique thing about my relationship with Irma is that both of us know the problem and it's very close to the surface all the time. Wouldn't you say that, Irma?"

"Well, it's *there*," said Irma, "but it doesn't cause a great deal of conflict."

"That's because, though we both accept and acknowledge it, we don't deal with it," said Walter. "Instead of conflict, it creates a certain amount of paralysis. It creates stasis." Stasis can be a form of security too, of course. "Look, you can cripple a person enough so that you *know* they're never going to leave you," said Walter. "That's the story of half the marriages in the United States."

The crucial difference between (male) jealousy and (female) possessiveness is that the former is sexual, the latter emotional. A man is worried about his wife going to bed with another man, a woman about her husband falling in love with someone else. Most of the married women I talked with were like me—I really didn't care that much who my husband had sex with—once or twice. I preferred not to know about it, and generally I didn't . . . until later. But a sexual indiscretion on my part, though explained, regretted, and forgiven, never *was* forgotten and produced a definite crisis in the union that went on for some time. This rule seems to apply whether the parties are legally married or not.

"You're talking about an area where men feel most threatened," explained a male friend. "There's always another man in the wings, so to speak, who can fuck your woman better than you can. I think it's the basic argument against infidelity in marriage. Permissive relationships don't work. I don't know of one that ever has." I pointed out that they often work if it's the man who is unfaithful, but not if it's the other way around. "A partial answer to that is that the man is more quickly aroused and more easily satisfied, if you'll forgive the m.c.p. implications," he replied. "For the woman it isn't just sex. . . ."

That's what men like to believe, but, in fact, for women as well it quite often *is* just sex. If the woman has a mate and is getting emotional nourishment from him, it can still be a refreshing change to have a friendly roll in the hay with someone else. It doesn't mean she doesn't love her man —often it makes her love him more, but her mate has a hard time believing it. He refuses to believe it despite the fact that this is exactly how *he* might put the matter to *her* if the situation were reversed. Extramarital sex, while nice, isn't that important to her, however, and she's usually quite willing to forgo it in favor of maintaining the security and trust of the marital bond, legal or otherwise, which is not, for her, primarily sexual.

There are men who consider themselves free, of course, and are not aware of experiencing sexual jealousy. Walter and several other men I talked with cannot endure the thought of limiting their sexual experiences to one woman, no matter how anchored they are in her emotionally. They talk of swinging, of threesomes and foursomes; this would obviate the need for deception and guilt and, presumably, give the woman equal sexual rights. However, the women were not equally keen on the idea. They pointed out that there were not all that many men they were attracted to— far fewer, it would seem, than there were women their men found desirable. The men were mostly impatient with this kind of reasoning, arguing that if the women were less "hung up" they'd surely find more men they'd want to sleep with.

But there is something else at work here. The men may

not be aware of the cichlid effect, but the women have a strong inkling that there is much that is being left out. For when, after much browbeating and blandishment, the wives *did* make it with another man and, God forbid, really *enjoyed* themselves, there was often hell to pay. What the woman is supposed to do is have sex with the other man— it's kind of titillating to her mate and proves how fair he is —but not really to dig it very much. And afterward she is supposed to reassure her mate that nobody, but nobody, can do her like he does.

This was the pattern for one couple I know. She went along with his program, reluctantly, until the day came that she *did* meet a man who moved her, and she really let herself go. And the husband didn't like it one bit. In fact, he was quite upset. Getting the message, the wife put a definite halt to *her* end of the swinging, though the husband still gets it on with other women.

To be sure, quite a few men *do* want to get rid of that gut jealousy, and this may be one reason why they want to experiment with group sex. Boris, who worried about his need for sexual conquests, told of a mescaline trip during which, he felt, he slew the jealousy monster once and for all. "What I did was hallucinate, in a most vivid way, watching my wife in sexual activity with another man. The love thing never bothered me, I felt so solid in that area; I know how hard it is to find someone who will stand the test of time. It was the idea of her body, this thing I owned, and I worked it out by, in a sense, *giving* it away. It wasn't sexually arousing, I didn't clap my hands. But I *saw* it—the tenderness, the passion of it. It was like taking medicine— a medicine I knew would make me well, and it did. Jealousy is violence. The jealous feeling that a man has for another man is to kill him. Who wants that?"

One might be tempted to congratulate Boris, except for the suspicion that the monster is not really slain, just gone underground. Boris's marriage did not, in fact, open up but went into a rapid decline—not over sexual jealousy but over competitiveness, conflict of work interests, and betrayal of trust. We know that if you get cured of smoking through hypnosis, you're likely to start biting your nails. Many people who swear they are rid of jealousy are only fooling themselves, so that the anger and resentment, which have only been repressed, come out in all sorts of strange and devious ways.

People tend to make *agreements:* we will have such and such a relationship, we are free, etc. Then, when they find they have not really licked the gut emotion and are suffering, they feel they cannot admit to their shameful failings, or do not wish to renege on the agreement. In one negative way or another, the frustration is going to come out. It's better to say, "Look, I know we agreed, but I can't cut it," and work it out from there.

Despite the sexual revolution, and the great availability of sexual partners, a surprisingly large number of people still marry, or cohabit, in order to have a ready and reliable source of good steady sex. This was brought out by one man (I shall call him Adam, and his wife, Eve, for those were their nicknames in Brazil, where he was in the Peace Corps). He is twenty-six, a schoolteacher; she is twenty-four and works for a women's fashion magazine. Both are very attractive, in a similar way—the type who occasion the comment, "Don't they make a lovely couple?" Unlike Walter and Irma, they presented a solid couple front. Adam did almost all the talking, Eve only interjecting a supportive comment now and then.

Adam cited a conference that had taken place at the magazine where Eve worked. The men surveyed had admitted that a major reason for marriage was to "get it" regularly. There was even the case of a man who, after his divorce, entered into an agreement with his ex-wife whereby he would pay her fifty dollars more alimony per week if they could have sex once or twice a month.

"In a way," said Adam, "the very sexual preoccupation of our time may strengthen what you call pair formation. The average guy—the man in the street, as they used to call him—is going to find, after a few disappointing and probably terrifying experiences on the open market, that if he can get a certain woman for X number of years, what a relief! His masculinity won't be put in question. He can walk by the marquee of the X-rated movie and think, I don't have to be a part of this. Or, I can be a part of this, I have a wife and can swap her for the night. But basically, she's his ticket into the world of magnificent sexual performance and limitless desire."

When you don't have to worry where your next lay is coming from, sex becomes less important, and less taxing. For the man or woman on the make, scoring takes up an extraordinary amount of time and energy. What we're back to is security. No matter where we range, in looking at love, or sex, or bonding, we always seem to come full circle. Dr. Rostum Roy writes, in *Marriage: For and Against:* "The insecurity of the median marriage partner about his or her capacity to do any better at landing a new mate is at the root of the silence which concerns the deeper failures of quality in marriage."

Another of the hidden reefs in the sea of matrimony is the assumption that love requires selflessness and sacrifice. In the first place, there's no such thing as selflessness; there is only the replacement of one set of satisfactions with another, perhaps more subtle, kind. Our concern over our loved ones is still *our* concern, involving *our* feelings of joy or sorrow, and what we call selfless love may only be what Aldous Huxley has termed "alter-egoism"—the kind of love typified by the self-sacrificing mother who works her fingers to the bone to send her son through medical school (today, she is more likely to work to send *herself* through medical school).

The alter-ego concept in pair bonding is often expressed in terms of completion, of two halves that form a whole—and not *just* a whole, mind you, but one that is greater than the sum of its parts. One woman compared the marriage partnership to the two wheels on a bicycle. Presumably, you travel better on a bicycle than on a unicycle—but only, to be sure, if both wheels are always going in the same direction.

If you're half of something, you are incomplete until you have found your counterpart. Although psychologists have warned us endlessly of the dangers of seeking completion through another, mythology and song, as usual, blithely ignore these warnings and express the way we truly feel. People in songs moon about being no good without him or her, of being lost without their love. But if you're no good without him and he's no good without you, the chances are excellent that you'll also be no good *with* each other.

Say you are unhappy and dissatisfied with your life. What's the solution? Find someone to love, get married, and you will then *give* to each other what neither of you has. The man is miserable in his job, he has to take all kinds of shit from his boss. But when he comes home, the little woman will make him feel great; she'll build up his ego and tell him he's wonderful. Or so he believes. The woman thinks, I can't do much, I'm kind of a boring person, but I'll get married and my husband will make me feel interesting and worthwhile. But as any computer can tell you, zero plus zero only add up to zero.

"I used to think I should marry because I need a woman to make me happy," one man told me. "And then I thought, Wait a minute! Happiness has to come from within—no one is going to lay it on me from the outside. People don't realize that, number one, they are alone. They must get to know and be comfortable with themselves. And after you come to terms with that, you can see who matches your individuality—for a few hours' conversation, or a lot of sex, for the different rapports don't always match, and occasionally you will find someone you want to live with for a while because you have so much in common."

Suppose you are not a zero (or don't feel yourself to be a zero, which amounts to the same thing) and *do* have a lot to contribute to a partnership. With your different personalities and interests and gifts you could form a great team. But in order to attain what Dr. Carl Rogers calls the "geared" marriage, where you mesh comfortably, you begin to lop off those parts of yourself that don't "fit." The partners supposedly complement each other, but it is hardly ever like lock and key. Rather, it becomes a case of trying to fit a square peg into a round hole. Women especially are alarmingly willing to cut off their toes in order to fit into the magical glass slipper of marriage. After all, once safely wed, you will never have to walk by yourself again.

The noble resolution to "work hard on a relationship" often means just this: I will do my best to get rid of everything that might cause disharmony or asymmetry. What you do then is "give up" things for each other. Of course, you're not really giving them up for each other but for the health of the "relationship." For how can giving up something you enjoy possibly enrich your partner?

The bargains are struck early and are mostly negative. "If you'll stop going out with the boys once a week, I'll quit wearing those skinny jerseys you hate," "I won't invite Jill to the house anymore if you'll stop inviting Jack," and other such trade-offs adding up to zero.

When the O'Neills made their plea for the kind of openness in marriage that would allow people to pursue their different interests without conflict, they were not taking into full consideration the extraordinary pressures exerted by a couple-oriented culture. A man and woman might well *prefer* to do their own thing—the woman might like going to parties by herself, for he tends to cramp her style, but she is afraid to expose herself to the contempt and ridicule of her peers. It is very, very difficult to be free in a vacuum. It is easy to say, the more people do it, the more it will be accepted, but who wants to be a guinea pig?

One problem with the idea of equality (which is likely to degenerate into an eye-for-eye-and-a-tooth-for-tooth) is that partners in a marriage bond almost invariably place different values on the various aspects of their union. The woman usually has a greater emotional investment in the bond. Consequently, her expectations are greater—and so are her frustrations and disappointments. She may be willing to make most of the "sacrifices," but in return she hopes not only to find emotional fulfillment but also to satisfy her ambitions through her mate.

Here we run into considerable difficulty. "I was brought up to believe that things you wanted out of life you got through your husband," said a thirty-three-year-old woman, mother of a three-year-old boy, who has been married for seven years. "You married a man who could vicariously give you things you weren't able to get for yourself. I have always been stage-struck. So I married a film producer. I thought this would be a great way to become involved in the glamorous world of theater and film.

"Then I found out it doesn't work that way," she continued. "*He* was involved, and I was home waiting for him to finish shooting, which is like a fourteen-hour day. He travels a lot and I can't always go along, and even when I'm with him on location, I mostly sit around in motels and wait. Occasionally, I've had the privilege of giving a party for the cast, but it's very frustrating to be an outsider."

What she did was launch herself on a career as an actress, and since then things have been much better in her marriage. Her husband is supportive of her career, although she feels he is unwilling to use his contacts on her behalf as much as she would like him to.

But this woman is something of an exception; others, less lucky or talented or directed, wind up deeply resenting the man's career and success. Often, they try to sabotage the man's work in various ways—to his great bewilderment and consternation. He does not understand that the woman had expected to partake of his success—at least by osmosis. Whereas what happens most often is that men caught up in a demanding career may well wind up neglecting their wives and children.

Enlightened self-interest is a far better rule of thumb than self-sacrifice, for it goes against nature to give up something without expecting something in return. "Reciprocity" means giving and receiving, not on a fifty-fifty basis but to each according to his or her own individual needs. One couple I know who have arrived at a way of life that permits them to do what they want are never seen together in public, though they obviously care for each other. She is very sociable, goes to parties and meetings; he is a loner who likes to stay home and read. When guests come to their house, he is pleasant and communicative. He simply does not seek out any social contacts. No one who knows them predicts imminent marital disaster. It is obvious that both of them are quite content with their lives. This is a couple that has been together for twenty years; one can only guess at what they went through in order to arrive at this amicable arrangement. But it does offer hope —people *can* rise above the social stigma of going their separate ways, according to their separate temperaments, and yet maintain their union. Whatever rapport or communication they have going in private remains just that: private.

2
Talk to Me!

We hear a great deal, these days, about "communication." Like "relationship," it is an O.K. word, modern and reasonable, conjuring up visions of people in bathrobes, sitting over coffee at the kitchen table, calmly talking things over. The two words together in one sentence add up to one of the superclichés of our times: "Communication is the key to a good relationship."

To communicate, however, simply means to convey or impart thoughts, feelings, and information—or, for that matter, lies (you can even communicate a disease). Nothing at all is implied about the *kinds* of thoughts and feelings communicated, nor about the manner in which they are conveyed. It is possible to communicate in words, in non-verbal sounds, or in total silence. You can communicate in gestures, or the absence of them (generally referred to as body language), and by signals so subtle and minute the only way to describe them is with the imprecise term "vibes." It is estimated that about seventy percent of all communication is nonverbal, and quite often this body language and/or the tone of voice may be in direct contradiction to the words being said.

The wife who screams at her husband, "You never talk to me, we're not *communicating*," is indeed mistaken, for they *are* communicating, if at cross-purposes. She is communicating her strong desire to talk—specifically, about the troubled state of their union. While he, by his silence, is communicating his determination to have nothing to do with her program of talk, which, he suspects from past experience, is likely to involve a barrage of complaints and accusations— an interchange, in short, wherein he feels he would be at a considerable disadvantage.

A couple I know quarreled violently throughout the thirty years of their marriage. They were certainly not repressing anything—they let it all hang out, and communicated like crazy. But it was the same quarrel, over and over. Once someone accused them of sounding like a worn-out phonograph record, and they both looked shocked. Evidently, the charges and countercharges seemed new and fresh to them each time.

Well, you might say, they weren't *really* communicating. All this means is that the school of thought which holds communication to be the "key" to a good relationship demands a very special, high level of communication. One problem is that although we assume we all see and experience things in the same way, each of us organizes and interprets experiences differently. We all know the classic stories, like the Japanese *"Rashōmon,"* of different witnesses truthfully reporting on the same event—with totally different conclusions.

It is on the whole question of what constitutes the ideal level of communication that men and women part company. Women tend to place a far greater value on verbal communication than do men, who appreciate the comfort of not having to spell everything out. (Truman Capote is reported to have said, "Love is when you don't have to finish the sentence.") This discrepancy in attitudes results largely from the different self-images we incorporate. Men are taught to be strong and silent; women learn early in life how to use words to attack, defend, charm, wheedle, cajole, threaten and ... yes, *love*. It was Kinsey who discovered that women respond more to words than to any other sexual stimuli (not dirty words, *romantic* ones). Five minutes of love talk is more effective than any amount of pawing (in fact, the pawing may have just the reverse effect), and it is a wonder so many men still don't know this.

A hundred years or so ago, to "converse" meant the same as to have sexual intercourse. The connection between talk and sex persists, and the popular songs describe the "sweet-talkin' man" whom all the women adore, although for other men, immersed in the *macho* ideal, he is somewhat an object of contempt. As a matter of fact, he may be an object of contempt for the woman as well. In discussing how she would like to see her marriage improved, the filmmaker's wife wished her husband were more inclined to tender words and gestures ... more romantic. At the same time, when she talked about an acquaintance whose husband called her long-distance to gush over how much he missed her, she said this man reminded her of a child crying for its mother. Although she longed for tender, romantic verbal expression, she also felt that no strong man, no *real* man, would stoop to such mush.

There are two schools of thought about what kind of information and how much of it to supply in communication between members of a pair bond. One is expressed by the old saw: "Confession is good for the soul"; the other is equally hackneyed: "What you don't know won't hurt you." Again, the choice made is largely a function of sex-role training. Men tend to feel that discretion may well be the better part of valor. Although women, in the past, have been accused of being devious and dishonest, today it is most likely to be the female who opts for the more difficult and dangerous, but potentially more rewarding, method of telling it like it is. Of course, she may *think* she is only being honest. Whereas *he* may think she is out to manipulate, punish, and control.

Though psychologists and marriage counselors by and large favor the talk-it-out approach, the more perceptive among them are aware that this method also has its drawbacks. "Total honesty is often neither necessary nor helpful," says Carl Rogers. But he adds that "any persistent or recurring feeling had better be expressed."

Dr. Israel Charny points out that many people can be honest only when they are angry. But what is said in anger is not going to be accepted, for to change anyone's attitude or behavior there has got to be good will. Nevertheless, Dr. Charny believes that marital fighting is "inevitable, necessary and desirable," and warns us to expect that the fighting will be dirty. Forget about fairness and consistency, face-saving or factual honesty. Since we always have this embarrassing stockpile of surplus aggression in readiness, it is best that the release of aggressive impulses, like the release of sexual impulses, be taken care of at home among relatives and friends, not out in the world among strangers and enemies. Seen in this light, some couples' lifelong quarrels can be considered a way to vent their hostilities and aggressions without damaging anyone outside the family.

One reason good marital talk is so hard to come by is that the romantic, companionable marriage is a relatively new phenomenon, and very little in our education has prepared us for it. The *de facto* segregation of the sexes in our schools virtually guarantees that we will grow up ill at ease with members of the opposite sex.

Be that as it may, there are problems and tensions that can be resolved only by talking them out. However, both parties must be equally willing to parley, which is often not the case. If it is the woman who wants to clear the air, she is likely to run into another facet of the cichlid effect— female initiative in verbal relations is welcomed no more, if not less, than female sexual initiative. In fact, such initiative is often punished.

What we have, then, is the irresistible force meeting the immovable object. "When a woman says, *'Talk* to me,' with that kind of intensity and desperation, she's really asking for something else," explained a recently divorced man. "It puts an impossible burden on the man because things, by that time, have usually gone too far—the lines of communication are down."

But if she waited for *him* to initiate the healing talk, she might well wait forever. "Why dwell on the bug?" my ex-husband used to say. His way of handling an argument was to walk out of the house, until things had cooled down. In time, there came to be fewer and fewer topics it was "safe" to discuss, and our communication became of necessity quite circumscribed, till it boiled down to: "You want anything from the store?" as one or the other was leaving the house. Predictably, when one of us got angry (usually me, since I had the lower tolerance of frustration), out would come "the truth," and it would go over like the proverbial lead balloon. I was the more articulate and my words could wound deeply—though no more deeply than did his silences and withdrawals.

This is the crossed-wire picture of marital communication immortalized by the classic James Thurber cartoons. "Well, *who* made the magic go out of our marriage, you or me?" asks the exasperated husband, or, on a more perplexed note: "With you, Leda, I have known peace, and now you tell me you are going crazy."

Against the plea for honesty and openness between partners are pitted the social facts of life: lies and deceptions, large and small, black and white, are standard procedure in relations between the sexes, acknowledged and accepted—almost institutionalized. (This fact is the source for the humor of most situation comedies from *I Love Lucy* to the "liberated" *Maude*.) All the women's magazines, from *Good Housekeeping* to *Cosmopolitan*, always give the same advice: act this way or that, tell him what he wants to hear, pretend to be the woman of his dreams. Men do it too, of course. "I don't feel like an oppressor," a male friend explained. "I'm an ego massager too. I flatter women and tell them a lot of crap. There's this enormous credibility gap with most people. The dictum is: Be Nice. What it really means, though, is: No Trust."

It is difficult enough to express feelings of ambiguity, never mind anger and resentment, especially when you don't feel you have a very solid thing going between you. How can you express your true feelings and needs in such a way that you don't threaten or seem to lay blame? The problem is not really the inability to talk but the lack of empathy between the partners.

As long as men and women live in their separate emotional worlds, they are going to have trouble communicating across the socially approved gulf that separates them. *Vive la différence* is guaranteed to keep us forever in a Doris Day–Rock Hudson comedy of errors and misunderstandings. Except that, when you live it, it isn't really funny. Sociological studies indicate that couples without children have better communication than couples with children living at home. The woman in a childless marriage is usually out working and may have much more empathy with what her husband is going through in his job than the wife who stays home with the kiddies all day. Sometimes, empathy may be delayed, as in the case of the middle-aged woman whose sexual desires now exceed her husband's. At last, she is able to understand the frustration he went through in their younger years, when the situation was reversed.

A parable of this classic marital development is the take-off on the fairy tale "Sleeping Beauty" presented on the children's TV show *The Electric Company.* Sleeping Beauty lay asleep for a hundred years. The Prince came and kissed her. Sleeping Beauty woke up. She arose and kissed the Prince. The Prince fell asleep for a hundred years.

Reversals of this kind constitute one of the main arguments in favor of serial monogamy. People do change, sometimes drastically, and their mates don't always change at the same rate, or in the same direction. And the changes in people are happening more rapidly than they ever did before—though still not fast enough to keep up with the changes in technology and society at large.

It may be that you meet a person at a certain stage of your life, and you're right for each other—you complement and understand and support one another. But as the years go by, the balance shifts, and you get out of synch. It's common enough to go from a size five at twenty to a size nine at thirty, to outgrow tastes in music, literature, and even certain kinds of people. There is no disgrace in outgrowing friends—nor even one's mate. For the kind of people who pair for personal and affectional reasons, rather than societal ones, there is no percentage in staying together in a stalemated marriage. "Loss of feeling for a partner is usually accompanied by loss of feeling for oneself—emptiness, meaninglessness, loneliness, despair," explains Dr. Carl Rogers, in *"Becoming Partners: Marriage and Its Alternatives."* "Divorce negates only marriage. A dead-end marriage negates life itself."

The women's movement has made much of the injustice of the system wherein the man is out functioning in the world, growing and changing and keeping flexible, while the stay-at-home wife, tied to children and housework, fails to keep pace. Whatever gifts and faculties she had atrophy. The husband may then divorce her to marry a more with-it woman (who is usually a good deal younger), leaving behind an embittered, no longer eligible woman with little training or experience for coping with life.

While this represents a true enough picture of a large segment of our society, there is also a contrary trend on the rise. More and more, it is the women who are outgrowing the men. They come bursting out of their split-levels, going back to school, going back to work—going backpacking across the country with an old school chum, who has also left behind a bewildered and probably resentful husband, grown paunchy and prematurely old in the dead-end job he's been stuck in for fifteen years, so as to give his family "security."

This new development is due, in large part, to the liberating influence of the women's movement. But it is also due to the fact that men and women, in our culture, develop in different ways. Boys are generally more rebellious in their

youth than girls, for society disapproves far less of un-
orthodox behavior among young males. Girls are more
likely to be the conservative ones, afraid to experiment,
inclined to hold tight. But as the years wear on, the man
begins to retrench, as it were; the conservative aspects of
him begin to come out as he reaches thirty or forty, whereas
the woman may grow impatient and want to break loose
from what has become for her a too restricting way of life.

Gail Sheehy, in *Passages*, her study on the predictable
crises of adult life, discovered that around the age of thirty
people undergo a crisis that prompts them to want to do
the opposite of what they were doing up till then: if they've
been keeping their noses to the grindstone, toeing the line,
they want to break free—perhaps even drop out. If they've
been foot-loose and adrift, they seek to take a firm hand
in their affairs and apply themselves to some work or
project. Thus, women who've been sheltered and underexposed may need to test themselves in the open world.

Among the people I know and have talked with, this latter
pattern seems to predominate. One such woman theorizes
that the men get tired out from hustling in the world. "As
they get more exhausted, the life force gets cut off. Whereas
women get a certain amount of security, at first, and things
coming *in* to them, so to speak. Thus they can learn from
life without being damaged by it directly, as many men
are." Perhaps it is this that is at the root of that famous
female optimism.

It is fascinating, sometimes, to watch the control change
in a marriage. Ten years after the ceremony the mousy
little wife who was afraid to open her mouth is cracking
the whip over her much-diminished husband. But being in
control does not offer much in the way of security, since
you're dependent on the tacit consent of the controlee.
Passivity, of course, can also be a form of control.

If marriage means commitment, we may well ask ourselves what we are committing ourselves *to*—the institution
or structure or *state* of marriage, which is static, or the
process of marriage, which is dynamic? Voicing one of the

main arguments *against* serial monogamy, Elizabeth Janeway points out that many people attempt to change their
lives by living out the same roles with different partners,
not by shifting circumstances into a really different pattern
which would involve changing their attitudes and taking on
different roles.

What the frustrated, dissatisfied wife gets is not a new
"relationship" (which she might have had in the bad old
days with an adulterous affair), but simply the same relationship with a new man. She might get as much, if not
more, out of taking a new job or a new course in college,
as she would by taking a new husband.

What we have to contend with here are long-ingrained
habits of attraction. We are drawn to people, and they to us,
for reasons that are largely unconscious and often date back
to some period in our past, when we became "fixated" upon
a certain physical and/or psychological type. Mate number
two or three, though different in superficial ways, often
turns out to be just like mate number one, in all the ways
that really count . . . the same weaknesses and strengths, the
same problems. Not infrequently, they even look alike,
though this resemblance may be apparent only to outsiders.

"For all the difference it made," Renata told me ruefully,
"I might as well still be with the first one. None of the men
I've ever been with would have anything to do with psychotherapy, for instance. It was always this kind of supercock
behavior, nothing flexible, nothing bending, nothing open.
They were very phallic for me, these men—very rigid and
erect."

Danny admitted he's been fatally attracted to clingy,
needy, dependent women—just like his mother. He claims
he's changed, that he's not attracted to them as he used to
be. *They,* however, are still drawn to *him* (it always works
both ways, of course), and he has a hard time struggling
against the pull of the old pattern.

"I have always loved intelligent women with highly
developed egos," another man told me, adding that he does
not like the burden and the guilt of a woman being too
dependent on him emotionally. Several other men, who also

liked their women strong and feisty, admitted that part of the attraction lay in trying to control the uncontrollable. They enjoyed the excitement, but at the same time their egos were constantly being threatened by these women, and in the end they had to let them go.

On the other hand, a thirty-four-year-old woman who has never married or lived with a man and doesn't want to, has always been attracted to what she describes as "male chauvinist father figures. Older men—strong men. You know, Gary Cooper. One criterion in the back of my mind is still: Would my mother and father approve?"

And Heather, who liked to prepare a candle-lit dinner every night, wound up with two men who liked to stay drinking in bars till late. Both were worldly and slightly cynical (not romantic like herself)—men who did not want to be tied down and demanded a great deal of time on their own. In a way, of course, they were "acting out" for Heather, who admitted that the lure of the bar was strong for her as well. "If I had the same job, and no child, I too would be out there drinking and talking to all those fascinating people."

"I thought it was just my wife," said the drunken stranger at the bar. "Now I find out it's *all* women." He complained they were all cold, nagging, manipulative bitches. I suggested, as mildly as I could, that perhaps it wasn't *all* women, only the ones *he* wound up with. To my surprise, he grew thoughtful and said, "Yeah, maybe you got something there."

It *is* possible to change habits of attraction. Becoming aware of the pattern, however, is only a first step. Some people do change enough inwardly so that they are not only able to desire but to attract a totally different sort of person. But the change has to be more than skin-deep—more than merely wanting another partner because one is bored and dissatisfied or infatuated with "somebody new." You can go through the motions of changing your life—take a new mate, move to a new city—and find that no real transformation has taken place, for you have brought into the new situation all the old furnishings of your mind: the same fears and hopes, the same blind spots and rationalizations.

What the pair bond has to offer, provided we understand that communication means sharing the bitter with the sweet, is the possibility of achieving true intimacy. "Freedom is not an ultimate value; human relatedness is," says sociologist Carlfred Broderick in the anthology, *"Marriage: For and Against,* but such pronouncements are shortsighted and do little to clarify the issue. Our needs and ultimate values change according to what our particular culture offers or withholds. When people lived in tribes and in extended families, they must often have yearned for privacy and sought to keep much of their inner lives to themselves. In our fragmented, alienated world, we long to share those deeper parts of ourselves with others. It is difficult to reveal our vulnerabilities to people at large, who may not expect or welcome such openness. So we narrow down our search, seeking the one beloved and trusted other to whom we may reveal the glorious and shameful secrets of our hearts.

Shakespeare's "marriage of true minds" may occur among people who are not married, or even sexually involved. People, in short, who have no social reasons for pairing (and sometimes, a lot of social reasons for *not* pairing) and who are together for the simple reason that they cannot endure the thought of being apart. But, as compelling and legitimate as the desire for intimacy may be, there are, once again, two schools of thought on the subject. On the one hand, we need that in-depth sharing as a plant needs water. On the other hand, intimacy breeds contempt—that is to say, withdrawal.

"Only by knowing another in significant and authentic dimension can we love, explore the potential of ourselves and fight off the alienation of our time," the O'Neills assert. At the same time they insist, over and over, on the importance of privacy, of not trespassing on the other's ego territory, explaining that couples attack and undermine one another's identities in thousands of ways, many of them trivial in themselves, but collectively very damaging indeed. Furthermore, like most psychologists, they warn of the dangers of two people becoming submerged in one another.

"We get the best picture of ourselves—the *only* picture of ourselves—through other people's eyes," one man told me. "You get a clearer and longer-lasting picture—neither overexposed nor underexposed—from someone you see all the time, over a period of years, than you get from different people who are only sporadically involved with you and with whom you play different roles."

Though he felt it was essential for a couple to live together and see each other every day, he admitted the danger of playing too limited a role with your partner in order to get back this simple, clear mirror reflection. Also, he recognized the tendency to build up certain habits of dissimulation—to protect your space as well as to keep the peace.

All these cautionary comments notwithstanding, the notion of marriage as a haven and refuge, an escape from the troubles of life, is part of our mythic heritage and will not be easily dislodged from our minds. In its zeal to free the Betty Friedan housewife from her enslavement, the women's movement has failed to give certain realities of life their proper due. Even a "good" job becomes a bore and a chore—and most jobs are not good. In a recent sociological survey it was discovered that by far the great majority of people—men *and* women—did not like their jobs. Many, in fact, actually *hated* them. What this means is that now, as in the past, a large number of women want to get married so they can *stop* working, at least for a while.

The woman is twenty-eight, let us say, or thirty, or thirty-five. She has been working since she was eighteen, or, if she went to college, since she was twenty-two. By most people's standards, she is quite liberated. Certainly she is aware of the difficulties of living in a pair bond; she's probably tried it herself, for a time—besides, she has only to look at the examples all around her.

Nevertheless, she's *had* it with working. She wants *out!* The thirtyish working women I know keep saying to me, in tones of desperation and defiance, "You know, I'd give *anything* to get married, stop working, and stay home. Spend my days puttering around the house, whipping up groovy meals ... maybe even have a baby. I don't care if it's unhip or unliberated. After fifteen years of rush-hour crush and office politics and indigestible lunches, household drudgery will seem like a *vacation.*"

Remembering some of the shit jobs I've had, I too would have done whatever was necessary in order to get out. Of course, marriage is not the only way. Many women, as well as men, *are* quitting the jobs they hate and taking their chances—going on unemployment, using up their savings, scrounging the next month's rent. But letting your mate share the load still seems the easiest way out. Even the men would do it, if only they could.

"I'd love to stay home," said Danny. "*You* get up at seven-thirty and hang on the subway straps and work your ass off—I'll stay home and cook. I *love* to cook. If I could find a woman who'd accept this arrangement ... oh boy! It would be nice if we could switch off—I stay home one year, she stays home the next."

It might be nice, but for most people it isn't practicable. Still, even if you have to work, it seems as if you get a lot more out of the time you're *not* working when you and your partner take turns with the chores. When you're worn-out, there's someone else to make you a cup of coffee and a snack. Fixing up the house is more fun when you do it together—even housework and laundry take on another dimension when they are shared.

Of course, you don't get all these benefits without paying *something.* You may set up your living-together arrangements as casually as you like. But if you are paired for any length of time, you will wind up with your lives intricately entwined; you will have acquired a lot of common habits, common friends—and common possessions.

The problem of dividing up the loot has been cited as one

reason for having a legal union, so that if you can't agree, the third party of the law can step in and decide who gets what. This is the same reasoning that urges marriage so that the man will be forced to provide child support in case of divorce. It proves that all the talk of faith and trust in marriage is just a lot of propaganda. Couples who live together without the legal safeguards are in reality exhibiting much more faith and trust—or, perhaps, only a more careless attitude toward possessions.

"I'm sorry, but that's petty shit," said one divorced man. "I can't see myself getting hung up on that." It may be "petty shit," but it's very real, since possessions have symbolic and sentimental value, as well as monetary worth. You can always buy a new hi-fi, but what about the painting you acquired together? To the emotional wrench of the breakup is added the humiliation of haggling. Quite often, both parties wind up feeling they've been had. Even when one or the other walks away from it all (usually, the man), unable to deal with the hassle, it doesn't mean he won't feel bitter or that he hasn't been ripped off.

The pseudonymous author of *The Homosexual Handbook* begs gay couples to consider a contract, some kind of legal document of joint possession. In a chapter called "Must you Marry?" he details the difficulties of what to do with the Meissen china or that darling little antique you both spotted at the same time at that yard sale, when the time comes to go your separate ways. The picture is vivid and familiar, but I cannot see how a legal document can help much. Things acquired in love and trust become something quite other when catalogued and inventoried on a paper signed and notarized against the day when one or the other will have to leave. Hearts have been broken over parting forever with a Siamese cat.

After all has been said—despite anything I or anyone else may write—people will go on pairing, as they always have and undoubtedly always will. Living with a mate is a statement to the world: "Look, I am accepted. I am loved.

I rate." Colette, well into her fifties, accepting her final lover, commented that she could not forgo the vanity of living under someone else's gaze. But perhaps it isn't merely vanity. Living under someone else's gaze makes us feel real, makes us feel alive—it keeps us from falling off the edge, from slipping into the void.

The satisfactions to be derived from pair-bonding are very profound. If I have not dealt with the satisfactions at greater length, it is because happiness, in large part, is inarticulate. The couples I talked with who said they were happy had a hard time zeroing in on the precise sources of their satisfactions. Some of them had evidently never given a moment's thought to why they wanted to be paired, it seemed so "natural" and so "right." The people who were unhappy, on the other hand, had lots and lots to say, and showed remarkable insight. Leo Tolstoy's oft-quoted remark—that happy families are all the same, but that each unhappy family is unhappy in its own way—was taken one step further by Virginia Woolf, who speculated that the world, as depicted in books, may look blacker than it is, because happy people are not much motivated to write books. They are more likely to be out digging in their gardens.

It seemed to me that the people who were coupled had less to say about themselves that was really interesting or new than did the single people I talked with. On the whole, the couples seemed to shy away from dealing with the complexities of their union. Perhaps they felt it wisest to leave well enough alone, afraid of opening the proverbial can of worms. Even in my readings I found very little that shed new light on the perplexing problems of pairing, despite the voluminous literature on the subject (or perhaps because of it).

Looking back on my own time of pair-bonding, it seems the happy years are all a golden sunlit haze of warm beaches and warm beds—nothing stands out very strongly. It is a little like those films where you get quick flashback cuts of the love affair: couple strolling arm in arm at dusk;

holding hands over wine in a café, et cetera. The painful scenes, however, are etched into my brain like sequences out of an Ingmar Bergman movie.

There is the theory that we repress bad happenings and recall only the pleasant ones. This may be true up to a point. But there is also this to consider: self-awareness and understanding and insight are tools, perhaps even weapons, that we sharpen only when it becomes necessary—that is, when things are not going smoothly. A certain placid air, a kind of slowness, almost dullness, seems to envelop the people who are happily ensconced in a pair bond; it seems to exclude all others and can be very irritating to the rest of us less fortunate mortals who must console ourselves with our sharp-wittedness, our insights, and our keen powers of observation.

It became very apparent to me, in my talks with people, that some of us are much more suited to pair formation than others. It may be a matter of temperament or of the kind of family background we come from, and perhaps, even a little bit, a matter of luck. Anyway, it seems some people have a positive gift for pairing, while others, just as obviously, would be better off alone. Most of us fall somewhere between these two extremes. For those of us to whom paired happiness does not come very easily, there are a few conclusions to be drawn from all this contradictory material that might prove helpful. One is the fact that people are less inclined today to accept living with misery, and will dissolve an unhappy bond. Thus, marriages, while they last, are more likely to be happy. In this light, even the rising divorce rate can be viewed as a sign of optimism, an expression of faith in pair-bonding as a good and viable way for people to live.

And so it is—at least some of the time, anyway. For many of us, it is not a question of either/or, but of both. There is a time to pair, and a time to be single. Some people who are quite content to be alone—who may even be pair-shy—fall into marriage inadvertently; the time and the circumstances and the person all come together, and that's it. Others who desperately crave a mate are unable to find one, or to keep one. Nonetheless, it makes us very uneasy to think that we might not have much conscious choice about our fate.

We do, however, have some choice about what attitude to take toward what happens to us. For instance, we could recognize that both the paired and the single state have their advantages and satisfactions, as well as their drawbacks. We could also try to revise our ideas about what constitutes a "good" or a "bad" marriage. A marriage can be "good" one week, "lousy" the next, "fair to middling" for the following month, and so on. Judgments of this kind are not very helpful, but rigid concepts of "success" and "failure" can be downright destructive—such values belong in the market place and have little bearing on the complex interchange between love partners.

Many people confuse a good marriage with a stable one; thus the values of success and failure seem largely predicated on duration. In pair-bonding, as in sex, length of time has little to do with the degree of satisfaction. People in general, and shrinks in particular, used to ask me, "Why did your marriage(s) fail?" I kept trying to tell them I wasn't sure the marriages *had* failed. They had *ended*, to be sure, but that was not necessarily the same thing.

If you have mated with someone for five, or seven, or ten years, and those years for the most part were interesting and rewarding, if the interactions and even the conflicts were dynamic and productive of growth, who's to say the marriage was a failure just because neither party was willing to settle for something drastically inferior when the winds of change blew too hard and too cold on their union? Perhaps the *really* failed marriage is the one in which the couple stays together for fifty years of boredom and frustration, and quite often, intense dislike.

But even here, we must be careful. Dr. Israel Charny, writing about *Marital Love and Hate,* has found that

> the nature and depth of psychopathology are identical for the husband and wife in the ... long-

established marriage. Indeed, a marriage may be characterized by strife and turmoil and appear on the brink of collapse. Yet in spite of continuing misery, one senses how necessary the marriage is for each partner's psychic survival ... the underlying personalities of the husband and wife ... their basic conflicts, their points of fixation and regression ... are the same.

I must also, in all fairness, ask myself whether my own marriages would inevitably have continued to disintegrate if they had not been dissolved. If divorce had not been possible, we just might have struggled through the crises and breakdown of communication; we just might have arrived at some kind of *modus vivendi*, on some basis other than the romantic one on which the bond was founded.

All intimate relations go temporarily sour at some point or other. If we hang in there, sometimes they improve. And sometimes they get worse. Heather, the romantic Englishwoman, told me that, during the five years of her affair with Raymond, there was a year or so in the middle when she was bored with him and was sexually turned off. However, she stayed with it, things got better, and the sexual interest revived. The second time this happened, however, it was the end. What this means is there are no rules. We have to play it completely by ear.

It helps to cultivate a kind of existential resignation and humor, however wry ... to accept the *I Ching* judgment of many life situations: "Slight humiliation, no blame." Don't take it all so hard! Too much feeling can be as devastating as too little. It's hard not to lose your perspective in a two-person bond, to dramatize and distort and lay blame. "So much of our thinking about human troubles still seems to remove universal existential or experiential dilemmas to a world of *pathology*," says Israel Charny, "or, worst of all, to see failures of human spirit as statements of intrinsic *incompetence*."

If we think of marriage as a flowing river, we can accept that there will be spots where the current runs clear and strong, others where it's muddy and obstructed; there will be rapids interspersed with stretches of smooth, placid water. When we commit ourselves to the river, we are agreeing to take a risk, for we never know what awaits us at the next bend.

The people I talked with who felt good about their pair bonds all had this tendency to go with the flow. They were not locked into roles; whoever did something best, or most liked to do it, did it; or if they both did it well, they took turns. They also had a kind of *laissez faire* attitude toward each other, and didn't feel the need to control their partner's social behavior. One of them might go off alone at a party to read a magazine while the other got drunk— neither would assume the social onus for the other. The most contented couples were work-oriented, busy with their separate careers and interests, and seemed to want and need similar mixes of privacy and togetherness.

In the matter of pair-bonding, we need to keep a mind open to possibilities, to allow for research-and-development. "A vast lab is being conducted, unheralded explorations, new ways of relating, new kinds of partnerships are being tried out," according to Carl Rogers in *Becoming Partners: Marriage and Its Alternatives.* "We are inventing alternatives, new futures for our most sharply failing institution." Unfortunately, these experiments get little public support. On the contrary, laws and ordinances, as well as the general climate of public opinion, are all geared to kill this budding laboratory, labeling the research illegal, immoral or "sick." We refuse to see that the essence of our lives today is change. There is even a degree of comfort to be found in the certainty of change, for it means we won't get too smug if things are going well, or despair if they are going badly.

3
All in the Family

Many of the benefits of pairing—the intimacy, the daily feedback, the opportunity for in-depth relating and growth, the nourishment for the spirit provided by what W. H. Auden calls "the Otherness that can say I"—can be attained through bonds that do not involve just one man and one woman.

With other bonding patterns, there are no reference points. No matter how good something feels at the beginning, there is no telling how it will all go—there is no sense of security. Yet for many of us, tying in with people who are not lovers can prove to be very rewarding and may exact much less psychic wear and tear. As we have seen, sex is not always the best antidote for loneliness—nor the best outlet for tension. "There are times when I am in a low mood, not keyed-up tense, but low-keyed tense, and sex just does not work for me then," said a young woman. "At such times, I have a great need to hug, to be close. . . . I can just squeeze someone and feel better."

In my opinion, people need to be hugged and squeezed a

lot more than they need sex, since this particular kind of low-key tension, which is close to depression, seems especially symptomatic of our times. You also need people to hug and squeeze when you are feeling happy and in a celebrating mood—again, sex just does not provide the right kind of energy for this form of sharing. The prevalence and popularity of the psychological techniques of the human potential movement—sensitivity training, encounter, and the "touchie-feelie" games—may be a response to these cravings, but the techniques don't really fill the need. The situations are too artificial, too contrived; participants are thrown into intimate contact without preparation, often without previous acquaintanceship.

It was my experience, during my brief foray into group therapy, that people would check their aggressions, suspicions, and reserve with their coats as they entered the therapy room—and put them on again the instant they left. For if one didn't, one was sure to get clobbered by the people outside who had not laid down their own weapons. There are really no short cuts, and life is not a game (though it may all be a Game, in the cosmic sense) to be played according to a set of made-up rules. To receive any benefits from human interaction, we must put ourselves out—we must make commitments, take risks, and assume responsibility for our actions.

We *do* need to form intimate bonds that have some feeling of stability, some sense of ongoingness, even if it is not a pair bond. "More important than marriage in meeting social, psychological and biological requisites is *family*," according to anthropologist Gilbert Bartell, writing in *Marriage: For and Against*. This family need not be genetically related. In many societies, the kin group is the most important element in giving the individual a locus in his culture. This kin group could include the entire clan or tribe; in rural areas, it could involve the whole community; in large towns and cities, a sense of family may be provided by the so-called sodalities—fraternities, lodges, religious organizations, etc.

Perhaps it is unfortunate that the Manson group chose to call itself "The Family," but it does remind us that there are all kinds of families, blood-kin or otherwise. There are not only happy and unhappy families, but good and bad families, meaning families dedicated to doing good in the world or—as with the Manson brigade and the *Godfather* clan of film and fiction—dedicated to doing evil.

Thus, when shortsighted moralists decry the destruction of the "family" (by women's liberation, the Equal Rights Amendment, homosexuality, or what have you), it is good to remember that they are talking quite specifically about the middle-class American nuclear family and totally ignoring the myriad other family arrangements that are happening everywhere—not just in counterculture circles but right in the heart of Middle America. When television, which is always at least ten years behind the times, begins to take cognizance of other types of living-together and different sorts of family setups, you can be sure these are no longer atypical and have been around for some time.

Until a few years ago, almost all the situation comedies on TV involved the American nuclear family in one way or the other. The television family was, inevitably, Papa, Mama, and the kids—and perhaps a grandparent, or other relative to lend some balance. The first breakthrough came in the acknowledgment of widowhood as a fact of life. Oddly enough, the series that deviated from the pattern early on all involved *widowers* ("Nanny and the Professor," "Family Affair," even, God help us, "The Beverly Hillbillies"). It seemed easier to believe that a mateless man might raise his children adequately than a woman alone, even though widows far outnumber widowers statistically.

Lately, however, we have not only widows ("Phyllis") but even a *divorcée*—with two teen-age daughters, yet ("One Day at a Time"). And there are other variations. "The Bob Newhart Show" is about a couple in their middle thirties—he's a psychologist, she's a schoolteacher—who have been married for thirteen years, live in an apartment, have no children, and, apparently, don't plan to have any.

The ever-popular Mary Tyler Moore is a *spinster*. She's well into her thirties, has never been married, but her life is far from blighted; she has her extended family in the people she works with at the television station, and in her neighbors. Offbeat families include "Sanford and Son," who are related, and "Chico and the Man," who are not. Shirley and Laverne are roommates, a classic bonding for young women, and let us not forget "The Odd Couple," one of the strangest and funniest "as if" families in the history of theater and television.

Whether or not we like these shows or find them funny, they are significant. They demonstrate that it is not only possible to live together in non–nuclear-family ways but also that such bonding can be as interesting, as rewarding and perplexing and generally human, as the more traditional ways we know. At their best, such unions can be comfortable and relaxed, offering freedom and autonomy along with affection and support. Of course, there are going to be clashes of ego and day-to-day irritations too. It is the petty problems, rather than the serious ones, which can really get on your nerves, and which can quite often be resolved in bed. (The serious problems are, as a rule, only aggravated there.) Nonsexual family arrangements provide no panacea, but they do offer possible *alternatives*.

The most common kind of nonsexual family bonding today is that between parents and children—or, more precisely, between the singular parent and his or her children. It is not a revolutionary or experimental setup because, for one thing, it is presumably not one of preference. Thus, the single-parent family is not seen as a threat to the established order. On the contrary, such a family may elicit sympathy and compassion from the neighbors, who assume that the members would gladly change their lot, if only they could. In the meantime, they are bravely going on with their lives, and making the best of things. At least, this is how the TV comedies present the matter.

However, television and the neighbors may not be quite

ready to deal with the trend to go it solo all the way. Unwed mothers have been around forever ... but not out of choice. Today, more and more women are opting to have babies without being married or even having an "understanding" of any sort with a man. "Old men come and go, but a child is yours ... maybe not forever, but at least until it grows up," said one young woman, who had despaired of the man-woman bond ever providing her with a sense of family. For many women, and a growing number of men, children offer the only possibility of any semblance of family life; quite often, children also provide their parents with an *extended* family of sorts, in the form of other parents and their children, neighbors, friends, and relatives who would leave the couple or nuclear family strictly alone, but who are able and willing to give aid and comfort to single parent and offspring.

When Walter and Irma and I talked about anchoring, I said at first that I no longer had an anchor. "What about your daughter?" Walter asked. I realized that, yes, she *was* my anchor—someone to give my life a particular form and purpose, to keep me from drifting; someone to whom I am committed more deeply and irrevocably than to any other human being I have ever known. Marco Vassi's definition of a "meaningful relationship" was: "If this person were to die tomorrow, it would seriously affect your life." Well, said I, such a meaningful relationship has been mine for the last ten years. He looked nonplused at first. Then he said, "Ah ... your child!"

It does not have to be a *child*, of course. The spinster portrait painter and her eccentric old poet grandfather, in Tennessee Williams's *The Night of the Iguana*, made for each other "a home, a family," even though they were always traveling. Such bonds were more common in the old days, when adults living with parents were not deprecated as "neurotic" and "dependent." Most of us, it is true, would not want to live with our parents, in this age of the generation gap. What I question is the across-the-board condemnation of such a bonding arrangement.

Michael McFadden, in his book called *Bachelor Fatherhood* writes: "Over the years I have lived alone, lived with male roommates ... with various women, lived with a wife and lived with a wife and children. I like my present set-up best. I have many of the advantages of being single and many of the joys of family life." He talks about his life with his three children, aged seven, eight, and ten: "We kind of review the day, talk about things they did, things I did." What seems to characterize the bond between single parent and offspring is a certain kind of camaraderie. You hear such expressions as "we operate as a team" or "we're real partners." The widowed heroine of the film *Alice Doesn't Live Here Any More* tells her eleven-year-old son, when he's acting up in the car, "we're in this together, you know." Almost all the solo parents of my acquaintance have this kind of attitude toward their children—namely, that they're *people,* junior partners rather than a subject species, whom one can talk to and work things out with.

That's all very fine and good for the grownups, you might say, but what about the poor children? There is still a widespread conviction that every child absolutely needs two live-in parents for its psychological well-being, no matter how antagonistic they might be or how much they use the child as a football in their marital wrangles. But extensive psychological tests have failed to prove that children from one-parent families have more emotional problems than other children. What seems to damage children is parents holding back on love, or else swamping them with it, and that can happen in any kind of family. As a matter of fact, the mother of the "normal" nuclear household is much more likely to be clutching and overprotective than the lone mother who is out working, coping with life, meeting people, and trying to work things out. Single parents are well aware of their children's need for other adults in their lives, and usually take pains to provide these other people, whereas the suburban housewife may feel the immediate family is quite sufficient. Thus, the household of one adult and one or more children is less likely to be a self-sealed, claustrophobic unit than the typical nuclear family.

Even at a young age, children seem to understand this business of we're-in-this-together and are much more likely to pull their own weight. Strangely enough, they don't seem to resent it as much as might be imagined; on the whole, I find they appreciate the trust and confidence the single parent places in them, and react responsibly. In many of these households the War Between Adults and Children seems to be less virulent; of my daughter's friends, only the ones from single-parent homes deal with me straight on and talk to me unself-consciously—the others "Mrs. West" me to death and won't look me straight in the eye, for I am the Enemy . . . a Grownup.

Much of the difficulty of raising children may have to do with the unrealistic demands and expectations of the nuclear, child-oriented family. During a recent TV symposium, a group of middle-class parents, from different backgrounds and different parts of the country, were asked whether or not, if they had the chance to do it over, they would have children. About seventy percent of them said *no!* Maybe they worked too hard at it—read too many books by experts, worried too much. It is interesting to contrast this response with the attitudes of single parents in a group I participated in for a time. Here the problems seemed to reside not in the children but in battling ex-spouses *over* the children. So far from thinking of the kids as burdens, the parents—in particular, the fathers—seemed to consider keeping the children a privilege and/or necessity for their own psychological well-being.

I also discovered that single-parent families learn early how to cut housework to the bone—how to organize life into things you do, things your kids can do. You can accept lower standards of house-beautiful when your identity and reputation are not tied up in the results. You won't get yellow-wax build-up on your floors if you don't wax, just damp-mop them, for instance. How many people do you know who eat off the floor? If the beds don't get made and their rooms get messy, the kids don't care and neither do their friends; and when they're learning to cook, you have to accept that they will make a mess in the kitchen. Something has to give, and you may have to adjust your priorities.

We all have different ideas about what constitutes being a "good" parent. Many mothers spend most of their time and energy keeping the kids neat and clean—then wonder why they are uptight and worn-out. We all know that love is not enough—in fact, love can at times be too much. Another discovery I made in our group is that whether the single parent was permissive or ran a fairly tight ship did not seem to have much effect on how the children turned out. What did seem to matter was whether the parent *enjoyed* the children and was able to talk with them fairly openly. If the mothers felt guilty about their life styles— boyfriends staying over, or whatever—and tried to *hide* things from their children, the kids always knew and managed to show their contempt in a variety of ways.

Again, we are dealing with powerful unconscious forces. We have seen that we tend to model our illicit and off-beat pair bonds upon traditional concepts of marriage. Our ideas of child-rearing are influenced by our own early conditioning to an even greater extent. It is amazing, and sometimes amusing, to observe sexually "liberated" parents teach their children what their own parents taught *them*, though they are often unaware of what they are doing. When they do realize the discrepancy, it comes as a shock. "I'd find myself saying things to the kids that my mother used to say to me and that I had rejected long ago," one woman explained. "I could almost see this balloon coming out of my mouth with these words in them, and I'd think, My God, am I really saying that?"

This woman, at least, may be able to do something about what she tells her children. But many others are quite blind to the fact that they revert to old ways of thinking and discarded morals when dealing with their children. "Do as I say, not as I do" may be the motto in unconventional households as much as in traditional ones. Perhaps this conflict between old and new values is one reason child rearing seems so difficult these days; it may be all right for us to experiment and break the rules, but is it fair to lay our uncertainties on the innocent heads of our children?

All love relations are fraught with ambivalence. "Love," says Fay Weldon in *Female Friends*

> is a force which keeps people revolving round each other in fixed orbit, and at a precise distance, as planets revolve around the sun; and the moon, that cold creature, around the earth ... it is certainly true that with the force which attracts us to other people comes a force which similarly repels—keeps us forever juggling in our inner spaces, like motes in a sunbeam, never quite close enough, always too near, yearning for incorporation, yet dreading it.

This love-hate polarity is strongest in bonds that are not easily dissolved, for social as well as personal reasons. The concept of for-better-or-for-worse, in-sickness-or-in-health applies far more to the ties between parents and children than to the union between man and woman. Certainly children have no choice in the matter until they are grown. And mostly, parents don't either ... at least, most mothers don't feel they do. So strong is the imperative not to cop out on parental responsibility that a woman at the end of her rope, who can no longer cope, is likely to attempt suicide before she walks away from her children.

This is a powerful bond indeed. A woman may now have more choice about whether or not to have a child but once that child is born, and kept, there is no telling what its personality and problems are going to be. Theories of behaviorism notwithstanding, mothers with several children are well aware that certain temperaments and inclinations seem to be a result of nature rather than nurture. Just how a child is going to react to a particular environment is manifested practically from birth, and the vast differences in the characters of children from the same family cannot possibly be accounted for by the minor alterations in their environment within a few years.

In effect, this means that luck plays a large part in how well we get along with our children—a horrible notion to throw out in the faces of Drs. Spock, Gesell, *et al.* But perhaps a little humility might not be out of order. It may be just as well that we don't have that much control over how our offspring develop. Sometimes, the "neglected" child is better off than the overcontrolled one. We may keep our kids away from experiences that we consider negative but that are in reality necessary to their growth.

Tremendous weight, tremendous guilt have been placed upon parents—especially upon mothers. Small wonder more and more people hesitate to have children at all. But for all the intelligent and creative people to decide to remain childless would hardly be a desirable solution to the problem of overpopulation.

It makes more sense to *have* a child, or children, at some point in our lives when we are ready to slow down a bit. Very young women have a hard time keeping their egos bounded, and their heads above water; they risk becoming swamped by all the changes and demands of childbearing and child rearing. You're supposed to be more "flexible" when you're younger—you're supposed to "grow up" with your children, but what mostly happens is that you tend to regress to the level of the kids. And it is not true that the young have more patience; quite the contrary—they think of all the good times they're missing.

Also, the more mature woman may not be as wrapped up in ideals and norms, having been around long enough to accept the real-life concept of the "good enough" mother—not the paragon of self-abnegation, patience, and devotion of mythology, but a human being who is flawed, imperfect, inconsistent. Kids grow up quite healthy and unblighted despite the fact that very few mothers ever live up to the mythic image. Our children are a lot more resilient, and a lot more sensitive, than we usually give them credit for. A mother who loses her temper and yells at her kids but gives them genuine love and attention as well may be doing more for her offspring than the parent who is always kind and correct, swallowing anger and resentment—which will surface anyway eventually, often in the form of giving off conflicting signals to a bewildered youngster: the words say "Dear, you *know* Mommy loves you," but the tone of voice and expression indicate Mommy would love to slam the brat against the wall.

We cannot assume total responsibility for our children's development. Of course, we believe we must guide them into some kind of structure. But guidance is not the same as control, or pressure. Our children are exposed to television, school, their peers, other adults. They also need to rebel and test their own strengths. They have to live with *our* hangups and problems, just as we do, and this is all right; if parents are too wonderful, the individuation that is a necessary step in growing up may not take place.

Not only do we get angry at our children, and they at us, but it is also necessary for the child's individuation and our own sanity that a certain amount of distance obtain between us. While we need to cultivate a feeling of friendship with our children, at the same time we cannot push the idea of being our kids' "pals" too far. They need their own space. They even need to be able to put us down a little to their peers, for this is a way for them to establish their own identities. It is dreadful for a child to be so dependent on its parents without some counterforce, some leverage—be it sassiness, wiseassing, secrets, or just plain rebelliousness.

Once my daughter tearfully accused me: I had said so-and-so, I had been unfair; I had embarrassed her in front of others. I listened and said gently, "I'm sorry, Nina. Nobody's perfect." She laughed and hugged me, and the "nobody's perfect" line has become a standby in our household. Throughout my own childhood I can never remember a single grownup admitting to being wrong.

If you want to know how hard it is for a kid to be truthful and open toward its parents, think of your *own* parents!

Sure, sure, you're nothing like them, you're not bringing up your kids the way *they* did. It's true that times and mores have changed. However, certain basic facts about parents and children haven't. It is difficult to be pals with someone who not only has all the power but who also knows so much about you (or thinks so, anyway). Your parents know all your weak points, all your inadequacies—they have so much *on* you, how can they be trusted? They'll be your best pal, everything will be nice and equal and aboveboard ... and suddenly, when you least expect it, out comes this parent persona saying, O.K., that's enough now, you have gone too far, remember who I am. The point is, parents can't help themselves. And neither can children. It's how the bond has been programed, from way back. It's all part of the balance, part of this particular form of love.

In short, though children *do* offer an anchor and a family, it is dangerous and inadvisable to have a baby because you are lonely and at loose ends (one young woman told me she was having a baby on her own because she was "bored"). Though there may be love, the companionship young children can provide is pretty limited. Of course, many women enjoy the feeling of having someone dependent on them—someone who makes demands on them, as Irma put it. The position of authority in which mothers find themselves is not the least of the motivations for having children, for it may be the only opportunity a woman ever has to exercise any power or control. This is the dark underside of mothering that we cannot afford to ignore.

If marriage is thought of as some kind of magical cure-all, motherhood is surrounded with an even more complex network of unrealistic hopes and assumptions. It was not so long ago that doctors and psychiatrists prescribed having a baby as a cure for female neuroses. But women who expect some kind of mystical peace and fulfillment through motherhood are in for severe disappointments. Children can provide emotional nourishment, purpose, and enjoyment provided we understand the nature of the bond, what it can and cannot vouchsafe—and peace is *not* one of the fringe benefits. As in other forms of loving, we are lucky if we can find ways to make the rewards offset the difficulties.

Women who resort to the "magic" of motherhood to give meaning to their lives are no more misguided than the women—single mothers, especially—who think of their children primarily as burdens. Oh, they *love* them, and all that, but they feel the kids cramp their style ... prevent them from moving about freely, so they can find mates or lovers. But it is not true that being a mother will ruin your chances of finding a man. Many guys like the kind of instant family they can get with a woman and her kids—they are, after all, not the fathers, and there is not the same commitment or responsibility. Such men might be fearful of entrapment with other women, who might want them as fathers of potential children. In other words, it can work either way, and the single women with children are not having any harder a time finding mates than the women without children. *All* women are having a hard time finding men, these days.

Oddly enough, the single mothers I know have more freedom than the married women with children. One of my friends used to watch another of her neighbors and me with ill-concealed envy as we arrived at her house, all dressed up, to leave our kids with her. I could almost hear her thinking, There they go again, those women, going out while I sit home cooking lasagne and minding their brats. She and her husband rarely went out—they couldn't afford it even though we neighbors offered reciprocal babysitting services—whereas we single mothers always managed to go somewhere despite lack of funds, knowing we'd go crackers if we didn't, if only to have a drink, or a cup of coffee, or see a movie. Of course, *we* thought our married friend had a good thing going, a nice husband, a comfortable domestic scene. Still, she was a great deal more trapped than we were, even if she did have someone there to share the load.

It helps to remember that very young children *do* grow

up; those first years of heavy demands over, a child becomes a companion—someone to go to the movies with, or
a restaurant, or the museum. Someone to travel with. I have
suggested, only half jokingly, to women contemplating a
trip to Europe or Latin America that they borrow a child
to take along if they don't have one of their own. Most
children love traveling, if the trip is treated as an adventure. My daughter, only five at the time, was instrumental
in getting us an apartment in tourist-jammed Ibiza that
had been refused to a number of others; because of her I
received instant, courteous treatment in a clinic renowned
for its shabby treatment of foreigners. What's more, she
had a marvelous time doing it—charming the natives quite
effortlessly and, in turn, being charmed by them.

The point is, *you are not alone*—which, freely translated,
means: you don't feel quite so vulnerable, so exposed. If
you are a lone woman in a public place, you are considered
fair prey—to bold, speculative, or contemptuous stares, if
nothing else. If you have a child or two in tow, however,
your status improves immediately. You will get hit on less,
by the type of men you can't abide, and other women will be
less hostile; people in general, older folk and public officials
in particular, will treat you with far more respect and consideration. You can be more open and friendly—talk to
strangers more easily, and they to you. You don't have to
wrap yourself in that sort of psychic armor single women
are so often forced to wear, which says to the world: "Don't
fuck with me!" The armor is pretty effective, but it also
prevents you from participating fully in the life around
you; you shut out others, but you shut yourself out too.

To compensate for the difficulties and duties, motherhood does have its mystique, so why not exploit it? Which
is not at all the same as being taken in by it, of course—believing in the mystique yourself. Still, one of the fringe
benefits of having children is that your footing in society is
somehow stabilized. No matter how screwed up you may
be, or how unconventional, you have *suffered*—you are a
mother. Don't knock it! Even the most militant feminists

respect the martyrdom of mothers, and hardly a meeting is called or an event planned without arrangements being made for free babysitting. Some of these advantages even extend to fathers. A man alone with his kids receives all sorts of assistance, from neighbors, friends, and even total strangers. A woman in my town said she had never picked up hitchhikers, but she pulled over instantly for a man on the road with his young son. He told her all the rides they had gotten were from women.

Communes, as a form of non-nuclear family bonding, have received much publicity lately. But when I talked to people about living communally, the climate of opinion was largely pessimistic. It just doesn't work, they'd say. It's too complicated, too difficult to sustain. It only takes one person to throw a monkey wrench into the whole scene, so that everything you've built up falls apart. Et cetera and so forth.

A few of the people who talked this way had actually experimented with group living; the majority had not, and spoke only from hearsay and personal conviction. Some liked the idea of communal life very much but doubted they could accommodate themselves to it. "I'm too set in my ways" was one stock phrase, "I value my privacy too much" was another. One woman was honest enough to admit that "the thought of other people messing around *my* kitchen drives me up the wall."

Others who approved of the commune concept on logical and ideological grounds nevertheless felt it was impractical. The logistics of accommodating the needs and temperaments of a large group of people present insurmountable obstacles, in their opinion. "Maybe if you're spiritually inclined, you can make it in a religious type of community," said one man. "They're the only ones that seem to work. Personally, I couldn't hack it." People see communal life as requiring a tremendous amount of discipline and structure —concepts which go counter to the American ideal of rugged individualism and "doing your own thing."

If it is true that the religious and utopian communities have been the most successful, that is because they are the *oldest*, in time as well as concept. They are also the most structured. There are many models, lots of tradition to fall back upon. The religious type of commune antedates modern marriage and the nuclear family as we know it, by thousands of years. The formula has been tried and tested: a strict hierarchical structure, many rules, and a common faith that transcends personal differences and conflicts.

But even such communities have their problems. Group living is, admittedly, difficult and complicated. However, I am not so sure it is any more difficult or problematic than the pair bond, or the nuclear family, or the ties between single parents and children. It's just that the problems are *unfamiliar*, different from what we are used to dealing with, and thus we tend to see them as more formidable.

There is also the fact that numbers of young people entered into group living during the sixties with expectations so unrealistic and infantile that rapid and thorough disenchantment was the inevitable result. Since there had been so little precedent, in our culture, for communal living and its problems, the young were able to center all their hopes and dreams around this brave new world, where they expected to find instant family, intimacy, and love—all on a silver platter, without a price to pay, without any flies in the ointment. Nothing needs to be planned, nothing worked out; you just share everything, keep the vibes cooled out, and all will be beautiful. This was the picture of the classic failed hippie commune, from Drop City onward.

These kids are older now, and may have learned something from their early experiments. The trend of the future seems to be the urban multi-adult household, rather than the rural commune—at least for the kind of people I have been dealing with. One reason is that the neighbors in rural communities often manifest considerable resistance and hostility to the experimental living group in their midst. Not only is there more privacy and tolerance in cities, the urban householders are not necessarily involved in the counter-

culture or being blatantly unconventional in dress or behavior. They are likely to be law-abiding citizens who are
either working or going to school or both, and the fact that
they are sharing a house with friends or having lots of
visitors or "boarders" need neither alarm nor outrage the
neighborhood. What goes on behind closed doors, among
adults who are not only consenting but discreet, may be a
subject of interest and speculation, but it does not threaten
moral values nor the sense of propriety, as do the highly
visible rural communes that have received so much negative
publicity.

In many older cities, such as Boston and Philadelphia,
there are brownstones and mansions far too large and expensive for the average American family. Rather than being
broken up into apartment units, which involves not only
considerable expense but, often, the ruin of the architec-
tural value as well, these houses are being sold or leased to
groups of adults. In the old days, large households were
the rule—at least among the well-to-do; the families that
built the houses in the first place usually had aged parents,
a spinster aunt, a young cousin, and a number of servants
living under the same roof. Today, such a household is more
likely to be made up of peers. In Boston, especially, students
are very partial to the new living style. Eight or ten people
renting a twelve- or fourteen-room house can live more
cheaply and in greater comfort than they can living in
single rooms or dorms.

There is apt to be a lot of turnover among students, so
landlords prefer to rent to young adults who are working
in the city and/or taking various courses of study. Such people care about having a nice home but are unable or unwilling to devote an inordinate amount of money, time, or
attention to the details of homemaking. Sharing the load,
financial and physical, is the prime motive, but young adults
also tend to form strong affectional bonds with each other.
Often, children are involved.

Some of these households are quite small, consisting of
three or four unrelated adults. More often, they are larger,

but they rarely involve more than ten adults. Eight or ten seems to be the optimum number of people that can live together, even in a large house, and not feel cramped for space.

Multi-adult households are not to be confused with group marriages, which are extremely rare. It is estimated that there are probably no more than a thousand such marriages documented in America today, whereas communal living groups are legion. Which brings us to the single most perplexing problem plaguing such groups, and the reason more people are not eagerly leaping in, despite the many and obvious advantages of communal houses.

It's none other than our old friend/enemy, SEX. Whatever code the group decides to adopt, there are sure to be difficulties. If the rule is no sex among house members, that is too artificial and unrealistic. Natural attractions *do* occur among people living close together—what are you going to do, force people living in the same house to sleep elsewhere? If the group consists of monogamous couples, it's unlikely that a single person will join the household. Even if there are no single people, there are bound to be flirtations, infatuations—all sorts of sexual vibes going on. The closer people are, the more they like each other (and presumably they would not be sharing a house if they did not get on well), the greater the chances of strong cross-marital attractions.

If the household consists of monogamous and nonmonogamous members, the former are likely to feel uncomfortable and threatened. If the group is sexually experimental and "free," there is trouble in the offing too. People *do* fall in love, as we know, and get jealous and possessive; they fall in love with people who don't reciprocate, or a loving mate may take a fancy to someone else.

Author Michael Weiss, in his book *Living Together*, describes one such household in Philadelphia that survived for two or three years. The particular combination of people promised a lot of conflict, as well as excitement: there were three couples in their late twenties and early thirties, one of whom had an eight-year-old son, the only child in the group: and three single members, all in their early twenties, one female and two males, one of whom was a homosexual. The couples had agreed to stay monogamous and the singles, at first, had their sexual activities centered elsewhere.

In time, however, attractions and repulsions, hetero- and bisexual, began to occur. It only took two of the young people to break the sexual rules agreed upon, and everybody else felt ripped-off. The couples especially, who had exercised considerable self-control, felt betrayed and resentful. Although everyone agreed generally on matters of philosophy and life style and, moreover, was willing to discuss problems openly, troubles arose from the fact that the older couples were more conservative and more prosperous than the younger members. The clashes of egos and interests made for an interesting, creative life, for a time... until the conflicts became too disruptive.

A more homogenous household, one I have visited personally, is located in a residential section of Boston. There are six bedrooms, a swimming pool, two fireplaces, and an enormous attic that can accommodate a large number of guests who don't mind mattresses on the floor or sleeping bags. The basic group is made up of three childless couples, in their mid-to-late twenties, who have known each other over a period of four years. All work, often at more than one job; one of the couples has a small studio in the house, where they do free-lance advertising designs. One of the men is a carpenter, teaches Tai Chi, and works in a day-care center; his wife is a dancer and a therapist. These people travel and go out a lot, to the theater, recitals, readings, meetings, and what-have-you. Most of the day the house is empty, and even in the evenings many of the people are out. Whoever is there prepares a meal, and whoever gets there before it's all gone eats it—latecomers help themselves to the endless supplies of cheese, fruit, peanut butter, and such. The house members are mostly vegetarians, so meals are simple and informal, except for festive occasions.

They have worked out the problem of chores mathematically, on a chart which hangs on the kitchen wall, so they know about their responsibilities well enough in advance to arrange a switch if they have a conflict. Withal, the house leaves something to be desired in the way of cleanliness, but it never gets really filthy and the people do not seem to mind.

The two single members of the household are a young woman who had had a love affair with one of the men before he married and who was there only intermittently (commuting between this house and another in Amherst) and my friend Anne, who, being thirty-three and never-married, felt herself to be the "oddball" of the group. Anne was delighted with her room, the low rent, the interesting and attractive people, the casual and relaxed way the household operated. She had become friends with one of the women in a dance class and was asked to join the household when another member left.

Since there were always lots of people floating around, friends, and friends of friends, Anne did not at first feel left out by the couples. But after a while she complained to me that she felt no closer to the people in the house after five months than she did when she first moved in. They were warm and friendly, as always, but the intimacy went just so far. There was a reserve, a kept distance among the members of the house, along with the friendliness and support. It was essential, of course, to maintain a certain amount of privacy, but Anne, who was looking for family, was disappointed. She found the in-house friendships too light and superficial, and after another few months, she took off for California.

There were also elements of jealousy and power plays in the house which disturbed her. The jealousy was not specifically sexual—it had more to do with status, importance in the group, the quantity and quality of attention. These feelings were never quite up-front, so it was hard to deal with them. Also, single people like Anne, who enter such living arrangements hopefully, tend to underestimate the power of pair-bonding, with its more or less subtle exclusivity, as well as people's need for privacy—for space of their own, both physical and psychological.

Though many people feel that living communally is not "natural," the yearning for community is as old and as basic as that for pair-bonding. The fundamental unit of society, according to Judaeo-Christian tradition, is the fellowship— the *koinonia* (Greek for community)—*not* the nuclear family. More growth takes place in an enriched environment than in a restricted one, and it is in groups committed to discovery that the most noticeable growth and development take place.

Sociologist Edward Wilson writes in *Sociobiology: The New Synthesis* about the wide variety of family structures found among the great apes, man's closest relative. They range from solitary adults and mother-offspring groups among the orangutans, to monogamous pairs and offspring in the gibbon, to large social groups of various kinds among the baboons, gorillas, and chimpanzees. Nature provides us with many different models to choose from, and indeed all these different kinds of family formation occur among humans in our culture, though not with the same frequency nor subject to the same social sanctions.

Despite the difficulties and drawbacks, there are undeniable advantages to living in a communal household. It is one way to escape the isolation and alienation of urban life. You have a home, a family of sorts, which means sharing a totality of existence, not just one small part of yourself. Being mateless loses its sting (unless you are in an exclusively couple-oriented household). You learn to share good and bad feelings, and to see yourself more objectively. You react less defensively when several people make a suggestion or criticism than if your mate does it. Living communally can be a great opportunity for learning about human nature, our own and others'—for experimenting with offbeat love styles (if that's what the group chooses) without secrecy or guilt and with the full approval of the "family."

Group living can take a lot of pressure off the pair bond, and sometimes couples decide to try such an arrangement in order to save their union. Jane no longer has to give up bridge because Joe hates cards; she can play with others.

And Joe no longer has to give up camping because Jane gets hay fever and insect bites; he can go camping with John and Mary. Children, especially, stand to benefit from being around a number of adults with various skills and personalities and approaches to life. Having a variety of models, both positive and negative, gives children more perspective and more choice. "Young children accept quite readily that their parents may at times be sleeping with different partners," says Carl Rogers. *"Children accept their world as it is* [my italics], especially when that world is acceptable to the others around them."

At other times, group living does *not* have a healing effect on couples with problems but, on the contrary, accentuates the rift. There are no rules. If a peer group of adults who think pretty much alike is less apt to develop internal troubles, it is also less stimulating and rewarding than a group in which pairs and singles and people of various ages and sexual inclinations coexist.

One general conclusion that can be drawn is that some basic form of decision-making structure seems to be essential. The structure can be very loose—more a matter of habits that function automatically than of rules; or it can be quite specific and elaborate. However, having a structure and a few basic rules is not the same as being regimented. In fact, some device, such as the rotating chart I described earlier, may actually allow the members a great deal of flexibility and freedom. Also, the basic rules allow parents to ease up on the policing function of the parental role; they need to hover less, knowing the children may well respond better to the advice and admonitions of other adults.

Another conclusion we can draw is that whatever ideas and ideologies we may bring to group living will always have to be modified in practice. There is no way to foresee and provide for all the contingencies that may arise when a number of unrelated people decide to live together. Ground rules must always be subject to adaptation—preferably by consensus, but also by way of exceptions, in the case of certain individuals, or certain special situations. Above all, commitment to a group-living plan involves the realization that there will be problems and difficulties, and the agreement to persevere as long as possible, in order to iron them out.

For the most part, the groups I know of are doing just that. It is true that few of these groups so far have lasted more than a few years, but that is no reason to write them off. Again, we must try to stop thinking of duration in time as some sort of ultimate good. Carl Rogers says that

> communes are at little psychological and financial cost to all of us conducting the lab experiments to determine what place marriage, partnership, interpersonal relations ... and social organization may have for the future. Our culture ... cannot continue as it is. The flaws and fissures ... are too great. ... Communes, with all their mistakes and privations and failures and regroupings, seem to be exploring the way.

There is, it seems to me, one crucial key to all these explorations which is rarely mentioned—either because it is taken for granted or because we are not much oriented toward this form of bonding: the factor of friendship. Like other forms of love, friendship is hedged about with myriad myths and misconceptions—not the least of which is the erroneous assumption that friendship is both easier and less rewarding than other variations on the theme of love.

friendship

1
Friends and Female

The Greeks, as usual, had a word for it: they called it *philia*, and, unlike ourselves, they held this kind of love in very high esteem. *Eros*, whose destructive propensities have been amply documented in their drama, left the passionate Greeks understandably wary. In our own times, we tend to make the mistake of expecting to find both *philia* and *eros* in the same individual. It is the mate-as-best-pal ideal that causes us to spend all our emotional coin on just one other person—an overinvestment that can easily leave us bankrupt.

Perhaps eros has been overemphasized in our society because we have lost so many other social ties, just as sexual pleasure is stressed because we have lost so many other bodily pleasures. "The narrowing of the world of physical satisfaction as modern man withdraws from his contact with nature has been paralleled by another phenomenon, the dwindling in the variety and extent of personal relationships and social bonds," Elizabeth Janeway writes.

Though we couple more freely than ever before, many of

us are aware that some of our most profound emotional
needs are not being met. Psychologists have discovered that
the inability to be one's true self with other people is responsible for much physical and mental illness. Dr. Sidney
M. Jourard, author of *The Transparent Self*, realizing that
his patients told him more about themselves than they had
ever told anyone else, was led to wonder about the connection between the reluctance to be known by spouse, family,
and friends and the need to consult a professional psychotherapist.

When we hide our true being from others, we tend to lose
touch with our real selves, according to Dr. Jourard, who
paraphrases Polonius's famous advice thus: "And this
above all—to any other man be true and thou canst not
then be false to thyself."

Self-disclosure comes, ostensibly, out of love and trust,
for the good will of the listener has to be assumed. Yet Dr.
Jourard and others have found that there is a great deal of
dissembling and secretiveness among family members. Since
the structure of family interaction depends to a large extent
on how well we play our assigned roles, it becomes dangerous to reveal ourselves. Even if we did, the others might not
hear, might not accept the revelation. With people we see
every day, we tend to close off perception; we have "fixed"
them in our minds once and for all, convinced that we
"know" them and that there are no more questions to be
answered. We don't want informational input that would
force us to re-evaluate our relations.

Any free and growing person is constantly changing, but
others can find it very threatening to be forced to deal with
the changes. Never mind truth, or even love—what people
really want is *security*. We expect our near and dear ones to
remain consistent.

The fact is that we stand the best chance of being truly
ourselves with our friends. We don't have as rigid a set of
roles and rules for the friendship bond as for other love
relations. If we don't live together or see each other every
day, if we have our separate lives and separate interests,

this is not seen as a threat—changing and growing, becoming involved with new projects and new people, may only make our friends more interesting to be with.

Our friends' quirks and foibles are accepted as part of them. I have a friend who eats scrambled eggs drowned in ketchup every morning. That's O.K. It's even amusing. But if I lived with him it would be: "God, I have to sit at the table every day, watching him eat that slop!" Whether or not you like the same foods is *important* when you're living together—more important, perhaps, than how well you get along in bed. After all, you eat every day—three times, usually. But you can have a lifelong, deeply rewarding friendship with someone despite the fact that your friend loves garbage foods and you are partial to brown rice and yoghurt.

Perhaps the different level of commitment is a factor here—we do not feel *responsible* for the behavior of our friends the way we do for our mates and family. We are not so encircled ... our identity is not involved, and so we can afford to be more tolerant. If we don't like the way they dress, or eat, well there are other qualities that make up for their questionable tastes.

There was a time when every hero or heroine of novel or drama had a close friend, a confidant, to whom secrets might be revealed, true feelings made known, so that the audience could learn what was really happening with the character. Today, the function of confidant has been lost in the shuffle of the modern world and, like so much else, is being taken over by specialists—psychotherapists, counselors ... *bartenders*. But it is difficult to reveal yourself to someone you neither love nor trust and who, moreover, is unable and unwilling to reveal a true self in turn. Dr. Jourard speculates that much of the psychological data acquired over the last eighty years might well be bogus— lies told by suspicious subjects to researchers they didn't trust.

Studies on self-disclosure confirm the fact that women reveal more personal data to the significant others in their lives than do men. The old *"talk* to me" problem. But women should be grateful; female role conditioning in this respect is a lot easier on the psyche, for men are programed to equate masculinity with low self-disclosure—a major factor in the lower life expectancy of males, according to Dr. Jourard. The strong-and-silent trip results in low self-insight and low empathy, which tend to make men incompetent at loving, as well as difficult to love. No one will know if they are lonely, anxious, or hungering for affection. Men are even deficient in self-love; blocked by manly pride, they refuse to heed the warning signals of their body and psyche, thus driving themselves into early graves.

The friendships of men have been sung and celebrated throughout the ages; the trust, loyalty, and support males offer one another have been justly portrayed as among the noblest of human achievements. However, despite the loyalty and the trust, men seldom reveal themselves fully to other men. They dare not disclose their weaknesses, especially in matters sexual, even to their best buddies. If a man *does* have a friend in whom he confides his failings, doubts, and fears, it is most likely to be a woman.

For women have always been able to be intimate and self-revealing. At the same time, they have never trusted other women, never felt they could count on each other's loyalty, even though many a woman would never have survived, physically or psychically, but for the sympathy and support of her sisters—as well as her mother, aunts, cousins, neighbors, friends. The women's movement talks a lot about the new female solidarity called sisterhood, but such solidarity in the face of life's trials and tribulations is not especially new—nor is it especially liberated.

It is one of the ironies in which our times abound that the early emancipated woman usually found herself without the solace of female friends. She felt threatened by, and contemptuous of, the seductiveness of the woman thing—hot coffee and warm, intimate raps in cozy kitchens, where all kinds of subversive thoughts might be expressed with impunity (since they would never be acted upon).

The emerging woman's wariness had to do with the classic, ambivalent nature of female friendships. Women have always been able to confide to each other thoughts and emotions they'd be at pains to hide from a man; the tears that confuse and exasperate him are accepted as natural by another woman. Yet this intimacy and openness are marred, and often completely undermined, by the ancient rivalry and mistrust that go hand in hand with the genuine warmth of feeling. Women, so the story goes, cannot be counted upon. They are fickle, underhanded, treacherous; they cannot keep a secret, nor can they keep their hands off another woman's man. If your friendship conflicts in any way with another woman's interest in a man, she will drop you like the proverbial hot potato ... she will deny you, not just three times but a thousand. When a woman turns against you, friendship may change into fierce hatred.

It is useless to pretend all these accusations are man-made myths. Sisterhood may be powerful, but the competition among sisters is legendary. As for women sitting around complaining about men, they've been doing *that* for ages too. My mother and her friends used to bad-mouth all the men of their acquaintance, but it did more to reinforce them in their victim roles than to raise their consciousness.

Doris Lessing describes the problem in *The Golden Notebook:*

> Anna was thinking: if I join in now, in a what's-wrong-with-men session ... Molly and I will feel warm and friendly, all barriers gone. And when we part, there will be a sudden resentment, a rancour—because, after all, our real loyalties are always to men, not to women.

This is not to deny consciousness-raising its time and place and value but merely to suggest that it is unrealistic to idealize women in the naïve feminist way and to think all our problems are in relation to men. The lesbians I talked with readily admitted that bitchiness, cattiness, and disloyalty do not magically disappear in an all-female society.

"A code of honor is a luxury which the powerless cannot afford," explains Carla, a thirty-year-old highly successful magazine editor. "When you cannot get what you want by direct means, you learn to be underhanded; you discard people when they are no longer of use, or interfere with your ambitions."

Traditionally, friendships among women have tended to develop along predictable lines. During adolescence (which in our culture may extend well past the age of twenty), a girl has an inseparable best friend with whom she hangs out, talks on the phone for hours, shares the heartbreaks and confusions of growing up. Later on, the girls may become "cruising partners," going out together to meet boys and men. Ideally, the cruising partner is not markedly better- or worse-looking but of a different type, so that the two complement each other and don't always find themselves attracting—and being attracted to—the same men. There is a rudimentary hands-off policy with regard to each other's dates. However, this code operates only as long as both women remain uninvolved. Should one of them get serious about a man, it's time for the other to shop around for a new cruising partner. The woman who is left holding the bag—stuck with the apartment they share, perhaps—may feel bitter, envious, and resentful. Or else the provisional nature of the friendship is well understood and the women part amicably. After all, it wasn't *meant* to last; you were supposed to grow up and apply yourself to the serious business of catching and holding a man.

Once you are safely married and have children, however, it becomes possible to form ties with women again. The friend is usually a neighbor, the wife of the husband's business associate, or the mother of a child's playmate. It is socially acceptable that hubby have his beer-drinking buddies and wifey have her girlfriends for shopping and gossip. This pragmatic type of friendship is also provisional and rarely survives the move of one of the parties to another neighborhood, even though the women might feel really close at the time, and swear up and down they will call and visit. The tacit assumption is always that women are not important, that only relations with men really matter, however frustrating and destructive they might be.

These attitudes *are* changing, and not only because women are gaining more direct power. We are being forced to re-evaluate our relations with other women out of necessity rather than ideology, because changed life situations have caused us to need each other as never before. Most women living and working in cities are too far from where they grew up—physically and/or psychologically—too estranged from their families' beliefs and life styles to count on any support from their relatives. Even the woman who is involved in some sort of "relationship" with a man might deem it wiser not to turn to him when she is ill or depressed; since men tend to be transient and uncommitted, we are inclined to show ourselves to them only when we are at our best.

Suppose you must go away—on business, or to attend to a family crisis, or simply because you'll go round the bend if you don't get off by yourself for a few days. Even if you have no children, chances are you have creatures that need looking after—a dog, a cat, tropical fish, or house plants—for it is very lonely to come home from work to an empty apartment, with no one to need you or greet you. And chances are, you will ask a woman to look after your creatures for you. You may not trust her completely around the boyfriend, but you know you can rely on her sense of responsibility for care and feeding.

Or say you are freaking out, having one of those periodic attacks of funk, self-pity, and despair that seem to be an occupational hazard for the solo working woman. Chances are it will be a woman friend who walks into your unkempt house, where you sit sniveling in your rattiest bathrobe, your hair unwashed; she won't shrink from the disgusting sight but will offer you a hug and a cup of tea, a tranquilizer or a shoulder to cry on. She'll answer the phone, which you've left ringing because you know the boyfriend can't stand you when you're like this, and make whatever excuses are needed—to him, or your mother, or your boss.

Perhaps today is your birthday. You've just turned thirty (or twenty-five or thirty-five) and you're feeling grim— you've wasted your life, nobody loves you, nobody cares. But your friend, whom you hadn't even considered as you added up assets and liabilities, remembered the day. She's brought just the right gift; she's got a bottle of wine, or else she drags you out for a drink. She's been there herself, and knows how it feels.

Say it's Thanksgiving, or Christmas, and you're in a panic about confronting an uncongenial, conflict-riddled family scene. So you get together with friends, other women and their children, cook a festive meal and have a celebration. This extended-family aspect of the friendship among women has not, it seems to me, been sufficiently stressed.

Carla believes women are basically stronger and gutsier than men. "If I had to battle for something involving real survival, I would have a woman fighting with me," she said. In a crisis, women are not only gutsier but also more compassionate. A California woman told me that a starlet she knew always had a lot of guys hanging around, but couldn't persuade any of them to go to court with her when she was arrested for possession of marijuana. And although they were not really close, this woman readily agreed to stand by the frightened girl when the time came for the case to go to trial.

Another instance of women holding together in nitty-gritty situations was told by Rachel, victim of the liberation void. While working as a buyer for a New York City department store she met Leona, a successful dress designer. Pregnant at the age of thirty-six, Leona decided to have her baby, even though she was divorced and the father did not wish to be involved in the event. Leona asked Rachel, half-jokingly, if she would go to natural childbirth classes with her. Rachel at once said yes. "When I first committed myself, I didn't realize how heavy it was going to be," Rachel admitted. "Not only the time and energy involved, but the emotional investment I would make in Leona and the child growing inside her."

At first, the hospital refused their request to allow Rachel in the delivery room. That privilege was reserved for the husband, they said... "someone who cares." Indignant, the two women wrote letters to influential people and got newspapers involved; finally, the hospital relented.

They also got some flak at the natural-childbirth classes. "The woman who teaches the class refused to acknowledge my presence," said Rachel. "The first day we walked in, trailing our furs, everyone just stared. All the women were in their eighth month and I was flat and skinny, right? This one woman looked me over and asked, 'When are *you* expecting?' I said, 'I'm not. I'm the father.' Nobody laughed."

But the main difficulty was with the pregnant woman herself. She kept saying, "I can't believe you're doing this." Rachel tried to tell her she wasn't sticking by her solely out of altruism. She was learning a lot, and gradually being released from her own fear of pregnancy. "There's a lot of physical contact," Rachel explained. "You rub her belly and stare into her eyes during the breathing exercises, to get her out of herself and focusing on *you*. It's very hard for Leona to look me in the eye. She kept saying, 'How can you feel what I feel?' And I said, 'I don't. I feel what *I* feel.' "

Yet Rachel may have come closer to feeling what her friend feels than any man. She has a similar body, after all, and until recent times it was always women who assisted with childbirth. The emotional strain between Rachel and Leona hinged around the fact that it is not only more blessed, but in many ways easier, to give than to receive. When you are offering, you know what your motives are; when you accept, you may wonder what will be expected of you in return. There was tension between Rachel and Leona because their association partook of what neither of them would quite honor with the word "love."

There is a deeper significance, beyond practicality, to the unprecedented importance that friendship among women holds for us today. In *The Way of All Women*, M. Esther Harding notes that in certain periods of the past the tendency of men to seek the friendships of other men coincided with a marked improvement in relations between the sexes. For instance, during the Age of Chivalry, when men congregated in guilds of knights, the European woman's lot underwent a marked change for the better. The ideals and high morals that characterized male friendships were applied also to women, though to a far lesser extent. No longer were women considered merely vessels for physical pleasure and procreation; during this period they came to embody spiritual and aesthetic values as well, and were considered worthy of respect and veneration.

The change in the emotional life of women has significance not only for the individual but also for civilization as a whole, according to Dr. Harding, for we are once again involved in a dramatic change of culture and outlook. Through centuries of masculine, yang-dominated culture, concerned mainly with discovery and conquest, the feminine yin values, which have to do with feeling and relating, have been seriously neglected. Once more, the time for change has come. Now that women are developing their own individualities, instead of trying to be all things to all men, or else rejecting femaleness altogether and embracing masculine standards, we are discovering opportunities for spiritual and emotional growth in our friendships with each other. According to historical precedent, this change in women should also help to modify and revitalize the relations between men and women.

Women can be the leaders and guides in finding new ways for human beings to relate to each other, for we are by culture and psychology well suited to explore this area of life. The various schools of psychology which fall into the category of the human potential movement are involved precisely in this task of righting the imbalance which has so long existed between the realms of thinking and feeling. If women are not precisely in the leadership of this movement (for prejudice among professionals continues), certainly the participants in the different therapeutic groups tend to be largely women. It is not that women have greater emotional problems than men, but we tend to be more concerned with and disturbed by difficulties in this area.

Women have a great need to keep the feeling atmosphere clear. We are seldom content to lay a problem aside, or to gloss over the difficulties, as a man might. Women need to come to a mutual understanding, of attitudes and motives, as well as behavior. Such an understanding can be reached only through a thorough discussion of whatever caused the trouble. This kind of working on emotional problems "both bores and frightens most men," according to Dr. Harding. But it does lead to the discovery of the truth, not so much of fact as of *feeling*. Women, through their friendships, are helping to evolve new values, a new consciousness in the area of feeling-truth comparable, perhaps, to the evolution of thinking men have brought about through their concentration on facts.

Failing to perceive the larger picture in which their relations are taking place, many women continue to devalue their affectional ties with females. To attach too much importance to friendships with women is deemed immature, adolescent—if not the suspicion of latent lesbianism, there is always the implication that women form close bonds *faute de mieux* . . . because they can't quite make the grade in the competition over men. This kind of thinking, being largely unconscious, is hard to overcome; moreover, it is reinforced by the current belief that only relations which are sexual in nature have any importance or weight. This may be one of the reasons the issue of lesbianism has loomed so large in the women's movement.

Suppose you don't want to have sex with the woman friend you love. That particular gut desire, for a variety of reasons (including centuries of conditioning), is triggered only by a man. Should you nevertheless engage in a lesbian relationship because it is the "right" thing to do? Does it mean you're *repressing*, God forbid, and it's time to come out of the closet? Not necessarily, my friends. Sometimes, things are better left *in* the closet. It doesn't mean you don't know they're *there*. It has become axiomatic that we all have homosexual tendencies, but we have all sorts of other tendencies too that we may not necessarily want to act on, being unprepared to accept the consequences. We do not escape the problems involved in sex by changing the gender of our partners, for sex (in case you hadn't noticed) has a strange tendency to complicate human interchange. Lesbians still have to contend with the ravages of passion—with jealousy and possessiveness, with ego and power trips, with the mysterious, unpredictable comings and goings of desire.

When there is no obligation for the mutual satisfaction of sexual needs, the bond can then be based solely on liking, mutual interest, and on that inner psychological accord which is the true basis for friendship, says Dr. Harding. Even if the expression of affection in a physical way is an integral part of loving, this does not necessarily have to involve sex. We all know how good it feels to hug and kiss a small child—the soft skin, the cuddly warmth of the little body give us pleasure, but we don't (on pain of being considered perverts) translate this pleasure into sexual terms.

In Latin America, young girls walk about with their arms around each other; they sit in front of their houses lovingly combing and braiding each other's long hair. As benighted as Latins so often are about sex, there are no lecherous implications to the affectionate displays of young people... male or female. Once I saw a Russian film in which two war buddies who hadn't seen each other in years embraced and kissed full on the mouth. There was nothing homosexual, or even sexual, about the scene, yet people in the American audience tittered. In our society, kissing and embracing become taboo, after a certain age, even among members of the same family. At best, there is a little peck on the cheek, a token hug.

Rachel remembers walking arm in arm with her girlfriends in grade school, but afterward it became a no-no. Another woman talked about meeting some musicians and their wives. "As I was saying good-by, one of the women put her arms around me. I didn't think she was a lesbian, but I couldn't understand how someone I had just met could feel that way about me."

Whether or not putting your arms around someone is a big deal, or has to have sexual connotations, is in large part a matter of upbringing. Marjorie comes from an emotional Italian family where, she says, everyone was always hugging and kissing and pinching. When she went with some friends to a discotheque and was dancing with one of the women, some drunken man on the dance floor made a loud, nasty remark about dykes. "You know what you do with a dike, don't you," Marjorie told him, unperturbed. "You put your finger in it."

There *are* women who feel they can successfully combine friendships with sex. Melissa, thirty-four, a Jane-of-all-trades who is currently running her own small catering business, claims to be somewhat bisexual, and she especially enjoys a threesome—a man and another woman. Easygoing Melissa seems able, consistently, to combine friendship with sex. Though she has several ongoing sexual friendships with women, she feels that "the women's liberation thesis that sex is a natural extension of friendship among women is true only in this sense: only if it *is* a natural extension is it any good. I have close friends I wouldn't dream of soliciting sexually because I know they couldn't handle it and it isn't really necessary. Where sex enhances the friendship, it is like whipped cream, a little extra—you get thirteen cookies instead of twelve."

Women in lesbian unions, however, are mostly into a heavy romantic scene—in fact, it may well be that they are lesbians for the very reason that men are less willing to get so intensely and deeply involved. What's more, a lot of lesbians assume roles "straight out of central casting," as one disillusioned woman put it, although younger women who have been less affected by negative social pressures, seem to conform less to the classic lesbian stereotypes.

Women who are leery of the complications of lesbianism,

or bisexuality, may have some basis for their fears. One twenty-three-year old woman told me that, since her recent affair with a woman, she has become as self-conscious with members of her own sex as she has always been with men. She is afraid of being too seductive, of misunderstandings. However, that is no reason for women not to permit themselves the solace of physical affection with their women friends, for such expression is liberating emotionally. "I like to hold hands in the movies," Marjorie explains. "It's comforting, it's sharing, and if I happen to be with a woman, I'm going to want to hold her hand. It doesn't mean I want to go to bed with her."

Along with the fear of sex and of too much emotional involvement, goes the fear of betrayal. "Have you ever had your best friend ball your old man?" asked twenty-eight-year-old Christine, when I brought up the subject of betrayal. After Christine related the detailed story of the friend "going after" the old man in question, I remarked that when your friend has sex with your man, it is *always* the friend's fault. We will forgive our man anything, but *she* is forever beyond the pale.

I then asked Christine a difficult question: Had *she* ever had sex with her friend's man? Yes, she admitted, but the friend knew about it and it was O.K. A little further probing revealed that Christine and the friend's husband had put the matter in such a way that the friend finally said, "O.K., but not in my house, and I don't want to know about it till afterward." One may imagine her private feelings about friend Christine.

The point is, all the terrible things we accuse other women of are usually things we have done ourselves, or are quite capable, under the right circumstances, of doing ourselves. Women are very hard on each other. All the evil and inadequacy in ourselves is mirrored and magnified in other women; we project our failings outward, so we can feel righteous about rejecting them.

At the same time, this mirror-image effect can also be a

source of comfort and a basis for alliance. "The love between women is a refuge and an escape into harmony and narcissism in place of conflict," says Anais Nin. "It is, in a way, self-love."

Perhaps it is insufficient self-love that makes women meekly accept a subtler form of betrayal, which is far more common today. Say you've been seeing a friend or talking with her on the phone almost every day; you've grown used to sharing the problems, the small joys and sorrows of your lives. Suddenly, she meets *him*! And you never see her anymore. When you call, she is distant and evasive; she hasn't time even for a cup of coffee, though she lives just three blocks away. You swallow your hurt as best you can because ... well, that's how it is. Three months go by, or six, and then she calls, in the middle of the night: he's just decamped, it's all over, life isn't worth living. She expects you to pick up the friendship where you left off, and if you act a little cool, she is surprised. After all, wouldn't you have done the same?

Carla admitted that, until a few years ago, she automatically dropped women as soon as she had a man. But she always felt vaguely guilty when she ran into women she'd been close to and wasn't seeing anymore. "I'd tell myself, she'll call me or I'll call her in an emergency, but she'll probably never have an emergency where she needs *me*, and I probably lost that closeness we had for good."

Marjorie said it was O.K. if a woman felt very insecure in a relationship or was trying to get one established. "I figure I'll give her time to settle in. But then," Marjorie added thoughtfully, "people hang in with such weird relationships."

Rachel also defended the disappearing act. "That man for that time represents a real sexual need that I cannot fulfill," she explained, adding, rather wistfully, that she'd dearly love to have an all-consuming affair that would take her out of circulation for three months. On the other hand, Rachel's pregnant friend Leona had re-established contact with a man she'd known before, and Rachel had actually said to her, "Even if this thing with Bob gets heavy, I hope I can still be the father." She explained this as an expression of vested interest in the birth of the baby. "At least I am at a point where I can *say* it to her, instead of letting the fear and mistrust affect my actions."

This is important, for as long as women are afraid to express their true feelings, they cannot see how they are hurting themselves, and each other, by taking it for granted that any man of the moment, no matter how marginal, should take unquestioned precedence over even the closest friend. If we thought about it, we'd realize that many of us would have cracked up if we hadn't had our women friends to talk to. Psychiatric help is not only expensive, but there is usually little love emanating from the professional. Whereas our friend not only *cares*, but empathizes ... she's been through the same thing herself, no doubt a number of times. Still, no matter how much better they make us feel, we continue to believe that it is a sign of emotional retardation to attach too much importance to the heart-to-hearts we have with women. But the date with that creep last night, which was sheer bullshit and game-playing and made us feel rotten, *that* was something to be pondered and discussed and brooded over for days.

Even if a woman really *does* value her friends, she may find herself under a great deal of pressure from the man in her life. One development of women's liberation is that men openly admit to being jealous of women and to seeing them as direct competition. "He has the feeling," says Carla, "that some woman is going to seduce you, and then you won't want *him* anymore." A number of women told me that when they joined a consciousness-raising group, their supposedly liberated husbands became furious, saying, "I know you're bitching about me, how I don't satisfy you anymore."

However, the issue of sexual rivalry may well be an excuse for sabotaging a friendship that is really threatening to the man on psychological grounds. "Men ... are still, for the most part, quite unable to give women the emotional satisfaction and security they can find with their women friends," wrote M. Esther Harding in 1932—and things haven't changed very much since then. A young woman told me of an ongoing battle between herself and her boyfriend. She makes an appointment with a woman; he calls, demands to see her that night, and insists she break her date with her friend. "Who's more important?" is how he puts it. She tries to explain it has nothing to do with that, but to no avail.

Things are even worse when there is a particular antipathy between the man and the woman friend. Marjorie said she herself sort of hangs around in the shadows, hoping the man will disappear. Another woman said she does her best to maintain friendships with women who've attached themselves to men she doesn't like, and she makes her position clear: I prefer to see you alone, so arrange it that way, or else we have to accept what happens when the three of us get together.

However, there are changes in the wind here too, and more and more women are refusing to be forced into an either-or position. One woman I know is very much in love with a man but nevertheless keeps in close touch with her female friends, explaining, "If, God forbid, something should happen to this wonderful relationship, I'm not going to be left high and dry."

Some might call it cynicism, some might say it is facing facts; but similar sentiments were expressed by a number of other women. Sandra is twenty-five, married, and the mother of two small children. "If my marriage were to dissolve, it wouldn't scare me," she said. "I know I can make it on my own." Sandra's friends are very important to her, and her husband respects her need to spend time with them. Sandra's closest friend is a woman her own age who has never been married. "It's true that Joyce is alone and having all these troubles with men, and I'm very domestic and secure with my husband," she explained, "but that's part of what we enjoy about each other. She vicariously digs my family scene, and I love going out with her— it fulfills that part of me that longs to be single."

Karyn, who is forty-three, divorced, childless, and works

as an executive secretary, said her women friends are the most significant people in her life. However, she tends to be disappointed in them. "I get ripped off a lot," she said. It seems Karyn *expects* a lot from her friends; she asks of them a kind of emotional fulfillment they cannot provide, perhaps, and inclines to see them in the light of her wishes and needs, rather than as they really are, thus practically begging for grief. "I feel friends should be constant, but they aren't," she complained.

Karyn's plight exemplifies the danger that women in their friendships may fall into patterns programed for another kind of love bond. The sexual elements of a friendship need not be acted out, but they must be recognized and acknowledged, not repressed, otherwise the libidinal energy may affect the friendship in strange and adverse ways. Aside from excessive demands, such repression may lead to quarrels that seem to have no real basis and are merely a way of "getting a rise" out of the friend—of giving the friendship a greater emotional charge. If the women are unaware of what's really going on, as is usually the case, it can lead to needless hurt and bitterness. It may even wreck the friendship altogether.

Women who live together in an arrangement where one goes to work and the other stays home must be very careful lest they make each other responsible for being "husband" and "wife"—or "mother" and "daughter" in emotional ways. The latter pattern is especially easy to fall into, since our earliest experience of loving a woman comes from our mothers. But where there is inequality and dependency— where one person is more experienced, more dominating . . . more "motherly"—there can be no true friendship. Whatever love there is will surely be tainted by resentment, overt and covert, by *both* parties: "Who does she think she is, bossing me around?" on the one hand, and "After all I've done for her, the ungrateful bitch" on the other.

I've heard the women's liberation line, of how creative women need "wives." But I can tell you, from personal experience, that being a "husband" is no bed of roses either.

A young woman of my acquaintance found herself pregnant, abandoned by her lover, broke, and about to be evicted. She asked if I could put her up "for a couple of weeks," and I readily agreed, for her plight seemed truly desperate. I was working in a publishing house and trying to write at the same time; Arlene would pick up my daughter from the nursery, shop, clean up, and when I got home, there would be a cup of tea and a did-you-have-a-hard-day-at-the-office kind of ready sympathy. It felt nice, but after a few months of enjoying the comforts of a wife (all but sexual), I saw that she had settled into my cramped two-bedroom apartment and was making no move to get her own thing together; she was getting alarmingly more pregnant, could no longer do housework, grew increasingly lethargic, weepy, and complaining—all quite normal, of course, but it finally hit me! Not only was I the husband, I was about to become a *father*. She deferred to my greater maturity and competence, and in return, I was to assume responsibility for her life and that of the unborn child. I simply was not prepared to handle it. I freaked, we had a scene, and that very day, she found her own apartment. I helped out as best I could, with money and things for the baby, but she never forgave me for "kicking her out," and the friendship came to an end.

One problem is lack of precedent—women aren't accustomed to relating as friends and equals. But we are learning, and catching on quickly. In my girlhood, when women went out together, especially on weekends, it meant they couldn't get a date. Now all the women I talked with say they would rather go out to dinner or to the movies with a female friend who's interesting than spend a boring, uncomfortable evening with a man who's not.

While most public places are still oriented toward male-female couples, and some bars still discourage women because they might be hookers working the clientele, or might be thought to be such by the other customers (at least that's how it was explained to a friend and myself), these attitudes, too, are beginning to change. As more and more women are seen out together, they may no longer get the worst tables and the worst service in restaurants, and men are not quite as likely to approach them, asking if they'd "like some company."

One of the most heartening signs of the changing times is the new spirit of cooperation and fellowship among working women. The old-style career women, who had to go men one better in aggression and competitiveness in order to succeed, usually didn't like other women and rarely hired them, except as menials. They feared the downward pull, the identification with femaleness and all the negative things that implied.

Not so long ago, if you wanted to escape the entrapment of the female role, you did your best to become a "man's woman." It seemed the only way to get ahead. I could have gone to an excellent women's college but refused to spend four years with "nothing but girls." It wasn't for romance I wanted a coeducational school, but because I felt men were more interesting, more in touch with what I thought was real life.

"Ten years ago, men *were* more interesting," Carla pointed out. "Power is interesting; being out in the world is interesting. Nowadays, most of the interesting people I meet are women." There is a charge you get from people who are on the upswing, who are growing and expanding. The energy level of women is high, these days, and it makes us exciting to be around. Not only are women more interesting, they are making themselves *available* to other women, personally and professionally. When I was younger, the interesting women were all playing the role of "one of the boys"; they did not seek out or open up to other women. But now there is a growing confidence that the women one deals with—agents, editors, doctors, lawyers—can be trusted to provide the best, least patronizing, most sympathetic service around. There's a feeling in the air that *our* thing—career, identity, fulfillment, pride—can only become easier the more women there are out there doing *their* thing, and gaining acceptance for their efforts.

Even television has begun to take note of this trend. In one of the funniest, most moving episodes of the often saccharine "Mary Tyler Moore" show, the heroine has a falling out with her best friend, Rhoda, and experiences the biggest crisis of her TV career. Sunny Mary is "more depressed than I've ever been in my life." Everyone they know works hard to heal the rift, and there's great relief and jubilation when they finally patch things up.

One aspect of the new female friendship has to do with the fact that the women making their way alone in the world can no longer be considered the rejects and the failures. Often, they are the most vital and enterprising, the most talented and attractive members of their generation. As we have seen, such women have a hard time finding comparable mates, and may refuse to settle for less. Many of these women could have married but refused because they wanted something different from the early, conventional wedding—they looked at the lives of their married sisters and friends, finding them dull and dispiriting. Such women, in their friendships with each other, may be setting new standards for honesty and openness in human interaction.

They are seeking alternative ways for people to love and relate, beyond the archetypes and stereotypes of customary bonds. Even with satisfying careers and plenty of contact with the outside world, women, by and large, still need to have close, emotionally gratifying ties with people. We need to be involved, if not with family, lovers, or friends, then with humanity at large, as were so many of the great women of the past—Saint Joan, Florence Nightingale, Marie Curie, etc. A man may live in a cave for thirty years and come out whole; not so a woman. This is one of the most crucial psychological differences between the sexes.

To tap the vast stores of psychic energy within us, we must learn to integrate the masculine and feminine sides of our natures. The plus factors of both—courage, independence, adventurousness on the one side; compassion, warmth, and flexibility on the other—present no problems and offer no real contradictions. Women are able to encompass all these essentially human traits. We are even able to accept the negative "masculine" traits of anger and aggression (in fact, some New Women tend to revel in them). But we categorically reject the negative "feminine" traits of cowardice and duplicity, for these go counter to our image of the liberated woman. While we deny these tendencies in ourselves, we cannot combat them, only project them onto other women.

When we are able to forgive ourselves, we may be able to forgive our friends. And as we find we can trust our friends, we learn to trust ourselves. Confidence and self-confidence interact in complex ways, and as we value other women more highly, we gain a greater esteem for ourselves.

2
Balling Buddies

English, which comprises more words than any other Western language, is extremely miserly in terms that describe nuances of feeling and relating. For instance, there is really no adequate term to describe an association between two people based primarily on friendship, which also includes sex. Not only do "boyfriend" and "girlfriend" carry implications of immaturity and frivolity, they have overtones of a romantic nature that do not fit the kind of friendship I am talking about (neither does the French word *"ami"/"amie,"* which is more beautiful and dignified).

Marge Piercy, in her novel *Woman on the Edge of Time,* describes a futurist society where people talk about their "sweet friends"; they make a further clarifying distinction between non-sexual "hand friend" and sex-sharing "pillow friend." I have chosen the term "balling buddies," which is facetious and borders on cute, in order to avoid the pretentiousness and ambiguity which dogs most of the language we use about the sexual and emotional interaction of people.

By whatever name you call it, such a friendship might

well be the ideal compromise between the excesses of
romantic passion on the one hand and the spirit-withering
inhumanity of impersonal sex on the other. The quality and
extent of the sexual interest may vary greatly; it may be
marginal and unimportant, or it may constitute the primary
basis for the friendship. It may seem strange, after all that
has been said here, for me to claim that sex can be a firm
foundation for friendship. It can and does happen, however,
and not infrequently. People may have a good physical rapport and feel very free and comfortable with each other in
the sexual sphere, but socially and intellectually they may
not have a lot in common—not enough, perhaps, to interact
much in their everyday lives.

Doris Lessing in *The Summer Before the Dark* writes
about an English suburban housewife and mother, neighbor and friend to the heroine, who has never been in love;
she does not understand what all the mooning and pining
is about and secretly suspects it is all a giant hoax. However, this woman is sexually very free and active. She has
an affair with a young Greek, a waiter in a restaurant, that
goes on for years; when he leaves to go back to Greece she
weeps, not because she is in love with him, but because she
is sad to lose a friend who understands and accepts her
peculiar sexual nature.

The words "understand" and "accept" are the key. Those
areas of life the sexual friends could not and would not
share do not need to be understood. It is enough that they
be accepted, and that there be mutual respect for those nonsexual dimensions. Sometimes, it is precisely the fact of
not living the same kind of lives—of visiting, so to speak,
across the border, in another class or age group or social
set—that permits two people to be so relaxed and uninhibited with each other.

In our everyday lives, we might need to suppress certain
aspects of ourselves that do not fit our social persona. A
woman of a certain age or class might feel constrained
with a man who is her peer—she'd worry that he might
think her too bold, too aggressive, too vulgar; her sexual

preferences, honestly expressed, might shock and repel. Whereas the younger man, or the man from a different social milieu, might well admire her and be turned on by the fact that, beneath the ladylike and rather square exterior, dwells this wild and sexy creature. She can be wanton, or earth mother, for a while, and the man, for his part, can express his more sensitive nature, his artistic and intellectual side without fear of derision, or of compromising his *macho* image, the upkeep of which may well be a must in his own social set.

There is the possibility—even the likelihood—that such a liaison, far from being sordid, might well encompass a great deal of affection and intimacy. Balling buddies can confide to each other things they would not tell friends in their own circle (let alone their mates or family), secure in the knowledge that this information will never leak out, even if the friendship were to end. What's more, such friends are not likely to judge each other by the standards of their own or the other's circle, but may bring to bear on the matter a clear and unprejudiced eye.

Sometimes the partners' lives don't intersect much because they are involved in careers or other interests which make heavy demands on their time and social resources. The woman writer lives in a small town; she works hard, travels around on lectures and promotions, looks after her house and offspring. She has neither the time, the energy, nor the inclination for a full-time lover. On the other hand, she's had enough one-night stands to last her the rest of her life. Her friend is a musician, considerably her junior, who lives in a nearby city and travels a great deal, performing in concerts and clubs. He is too absorbed in his career for a serious love affair, and groupies turn him off. The two see each other when they can—two weekends a month, perhaps. Aside from the sex, they take an interest in one another's work (no competition here) and compare notes on certain problems: the private life versus show biz; the vicissitudes of chasing after the bitch goddess success while trying to maintain an attitude of integrity toward one's art. They share enjoyment of food, music, nature, movies. For the rest, there's no mind-fucking—they make no demands, do not try to change each other, do not pretend to feelings that don't exist.

Of course, such friendship lacks the intensity of a true-blue love affair. Nor can the friends be there for each other whenever loneliness or sexual hunger prevails. Many areas of their lives are, of necessity, completely unknown to the other. However, they are both grateful for what they *do* have, for there is love of a sort between them, even if there is no longing or pining, and the sex is sweet and good.

In the past, and to a lesser extent still today, men would often find this kind of friendship among "women of easy virtue," as they used to be called. With their mistresses, or with courtesans, men might drop their masks and relax; they could be themselves, show their weaknesses, their angers and sorrows, and their true sexual nature. They need not project onto those women virtues and frailties they did not possess and, in turn, be forced to comply with rigid standards of masculinity. That corniest of stereotypes, the "prostitute with the heart of gold," may have originated as a paean of appreciation to the kind of professional who offered sexual service in a spirit of easy camaraderie.

An example of this type of woman was portrayed by Melina Mercouri in the film *Never on Sunday*. The prostitute's pride and very identity were tied up with the fact that her clients were her *friends;* they came to visit on Sunday, her day off, bringing gifts and taking her to the theater, because they *liked* her. A real-life woman of my acquaintance, who used to work as a hooker in Puerto Rico, was very successful and earned more money than the other girls on her beat despite the fact that she was older than most of them and fifty pounds overweight. "I treated them like human beings," she explained. "I didn't make them feel like shit. They'd talk to me and show me pictures of their kids."

As with pair bonding, some people are better suited than others, by temperament and outlook, to be successful at forming sexual friendships. The type of persons who appreciate the low-pressure, low-key kind of sex that is most characteristic of pillow friendship are apt not to attach great emotional weight to sex. The primitive, subterranean layers of their beings are not tapped. They may find sex pleasurable—in fact, they may be very free and uninhibited, engaging in bisexual and other "polymorphous perverse" activities without any qualms—but they may find it hard to understand why everyone else makes such a fuss about it. Such an approach, though currently advocated as "healthy" and "with-it," is not necessarily the only one, nor the best, for people whose emotional make-up is more intense. There is no value judgment here: different strokes for different folks, as the popular song prescribes.

One woman's description of her relationship with someone she's been close to for years might well serve as model for the classical balling-buddy bond: "We have been lovers and may be again, but in the meantime we talk on the phone and go to the movies together. If all conditions are go, which hasn't happened for a while, we will no doubt have sex again. Meanwhile, there's no sweat and no pressure."

Quite a few extramarital affairs may be of this order. Here, sex is *not* the prime basis for friendship. The people may move in the same social circles and see each other all the time; they have a friendship based on other mutual interests. Upon learning that a married man and a divorced woman living in the same small town had had an ongoing sexual relation for years, their mutual friends expressed astonishment and shock. How, they wondered, could they keep such a secret for so long? Well, it seems the sex, when it happened, did not loom very large in their lives. "It's almost as if it weren't there," the man explained. "We're like a couple of five-year-olds, or something. We giggle a lot."

Why bother with the sex at all, then, people of a different temperament might ask. But who is to say that the affectionate playfulness, the camaraderie, might not be a source of great comfort and perhaps relief from heavier commitments? We cannot know what nourishment these people derived from their seemingly frivolous dalliance. When it comes to love and sex, it helps to keep an open mind, and not to project our own prejudices upon others.

For instance, there is a certain type of man who makes an ideal balling buddy; preconceptions lead us to confuse him with the stud or Casanova. This man, too, is apt to be described as a "good lover," but here we are not talking about technique (though that is usually not lacking) but of a quality known in music as "soul"—a quality of genuine emotion. In sex as in music, almost everyone can learn the basics, and there are people who acquire a degree of technical expertise and succeed in faking it, more or less successfully, all their lives. But as the old jazz song says, "It don't mean a thing, if it ain't got that swing." The strength of the drive, or the frequency of the activity, are quite irrelevant—either you've got it or you don't.

When a woman encounters a man who possesses this gift, she usually falls in love and tries to program the sexual connection into a "relationship." However, the man whose erotic sensibilities are highly developed is not necessarily monogamous by nature—quite the contrary. I am not talking about the Don Juan who either fakes it or abuses his gifts in the service of money and power, lying about his feelings to gain his ends. The kind of man I'm describing loves sex too much, and has too much respect for its power, to play games with it. He is usually a loner, and the sexual connection is his way of loving, of communicating and participating in the life around him. He may have a strict hands-off policy regarding his deepest emotions, but he's able to provide friendship—that is to say, liking and affection and respect—along with the good, true sexual connection. He is so independent, so secure in his emotional center, that he is not afraid of women and can afford to sympathize with and understand the plight of the many ladies who troop through his apartment or studio.

I know two such men—one is a sculptor, the other a jazz musician—who have been a godsend to many a New

Woman, caught up in the questions of modern love. Both men are dedicated to their art, which engages their most profound feelings, and to which they devote most of their waking hours. The rest of the time they like to make love. The women of their acquaintance, who are growing more sisterly and generous in common deprivation, often pass the word around: Call up So-and-So, tell him I gave you his number, he'll be delighted. He'll leave your head strictly alone, just good solid sex, and afterward it's friendly and comfortable.

The majority of women, however, find it hard to accept that friendship fucking may be one of the consolations of our confused and frustrating times. Not infrequently, women experience themselves sexually, in the most complete way, with balling buddies, for with them they need not be afraid to let themselves go. At the same time, however, they're likely to be mooning and stewing over somebody else, someone they're having a "thing" with, even if the sex is not so hot, or maybe even not there at all. For sex, no matter how good, is not enough—never enough without the mind-fuck, the thrust of the emotional imagination.

There is a kind of puritanism at work here: it seems somehow immoral and wanton to enjoy sex and to have magnificent orgasms with someone who isn't "ours alone." Even when there is affection and laughter and compassion (which might be lacking in a romantic involvement, for people often fall in love with someone they don't really *like*), we wince inwardly, we feel we have sold out, when we think of "all those others." The aforementioned jazz musician, especially, ran into repeated trouble with women who, despite his honesty in making his position clear, insisted on falling madly in love with him and making scenes in the clubs where he played.

With the others, who understand where it's at, it works something like this: A month or two might go by during which you see each other and merely exchange the greetings and small talk you would with your other friends. Then one day once again your eyes meet, and there is a spark: contact has been made and you smile at each other in acknowledgment of the mutual message: *"Yes!* Let's make love tonight!"

Not your cup of tea? No reason why it should be. Admittedly, friendship sex is not for everybody. Women are more likely than men to reject it out of hand, on ethical grounds, though they may not put it that way. "Not for me, it doesn't fill the bill," they tell you frankly. "With me, it's all or nothing at all." Marjorie said it was O.K. for it to start that way, but that if it doesn't develop into something else, a *relationship* (that is, an exclusive, committed deal), than she wants no part of it after a while. "The insecurity is just too great," Carla admitted. "You've got to hold back too much. You've got nothing to *build* upon."

Men, on the other hand, are very partial to the *idea* of being balling buddies. They like the thought of all that freedom—no hang-ups, no commitments, how lovely! However, that doesn't mean they can handle it in practice. The man may not want to get involved himself, but it bothers him if *you* don't want to get involved. Oh, he professes the same thing as all the others—Who wants a woman who gets too serious? . . . tears, recriminations, what a drag. But suppose you *don't* behave that way. He says things like, "You may want me, but you don't really need me. What's-her-face *needs* me." And back he goes to What's-her-face, who has promised to slash her wrists should he depart for good.

Another guy will say, "I know you enjoy being with me, but if I walked out and you never saw me again, I have the feeling it wouldn't really matter." He's likely to think, as he walks out the door, There's no place for me in her life, she doesn't give a shit; she won't sit by the phone and sweat it. The latter may be true, but it doesn't mean you don't give a shit. You may be very fond of him and look forward to the next meeting.

It has to do with that old male hang-up: the thought that another man might do as well, which is so disturbing. That is why one male friend is leery of combining sex with friendship. "I've known this woman for many years," he said. "In many ways, she's my closest friend. We talk to each other openly; she cries on my shoulder, I cry on hers. We've never slept with each other and we talked about this. We both feel it might spoil a beautiful friendship, because you get into the bag of doing things to impress the other, to influence their opinion of you."

Sexual friendship is not an "easy way out," as many people, especially men, are inclined to believe. On the contrary, it is very difficult, and requires a good deal of discipline, honesty, and awareness on the part of the participants. The tendency is always to slip into the old patterns, not only because they are familiar and accepted, but because they *do* trigger biological urges and satisfy primitive desires. "In her close relations with men," says M. Esther Harding in *The Way of All Women,* "a woman is always tempted to play the part of anima." (This term, as used by C. G. Jung, refers to the unassimilated, unconscious aspects of a man's psyche which he projects upon a woman; the female's psyche projected upon a man Jung called animus.)

The man has an ideal, conscious or otherwise, of what a woman should be and how she should react to him. If she does not conform to this pattern, he will try to force her into it—or else he will have none of her. The woman feels compelled by his set purpose, and by her own inner promptings, to give him what he wants and try to fit herself to his requirements. This tendency is reinforced by her own relation to her animus, which causes her to look for the ideal man of her imagination just over the horizon. Dr. Harding calls him the Ghostly Lover, who lures the woman to follow him into the clouds, and neglect what is here and now. "Her instinct to play *anima* to the man and her own inner tendency to follow the Ghostly Lover keep the relation between man and woman *unreal,*" writes Dr. Harding.

Thus, people who start out as balling buddies often end up "escalating" into a full-fledged affair . . . or else they lose interest in each other sexually. While everything is pleasant and comfortable, there is not the excitement, the *Sturm und Drang* which we have come to expect, and without which the erotic drive sputters to a halt; the sexual imagination feeds to a large extent on mystery, and—oh, paradox of paradoxes—on *insecurity*. Will she or won't she? He loves me, he loves me not.

Sexual friendship, therefore, tends to be a stopgap—a way to still the craving for sex and affection "until the real thing comes along." Again, we must try not set up duration as an ultimate value. This form of loving is still so new, so experimental, that it will be difficult to sustain for long. Furthermore, there is not necessarily a hard and fast line that can always be drawn between sexual friendship and romantic love. Many modern "relationships" are of a hybrid nature, and partake in some measure of both.

The permutations are infinite. You may start out as friends, have a sexual scene for a while, then end up "just friends" again. Former lovers—even former husbands and wives—may turn into "pillow friends" or "hand friends." Erstwhile lovers and balling buddies can be your stanchest allies—friends of a particularly trustworthy kind, since you've already survived the tricky sexual phase. An interesting instance of such a development is shown in Ingmar Bergman's film *Scenes from a Marriage*. For ten years, the couple never level with each other but sweep everything under the rug; when they are getting divorced, they start letting it all hang out, the anger, the bitterness—and the sexual passion. In time, when they are both remarried, they become good friends—balling buddies—who have weekend assignations in deserted country houses. There is no longer anything at stake, nothing to lose, and they are able to love each other with a freedom and gentleness and honesty that was lacking during their marriage.

Nowadays, there are more opportunities for men and women to befriend each other than ever before. They are working together, studying together, and seeing each other not in the hopped-up, sexually charged atmosphere of a

party or a social evening but in their everyday garb and
as their everyday selves. Thrown into daily contact, such
people are likely to get to know each other very well—too
well, perhaps, to sustain the classic anima-animus fantasy.
Friendships based on shared ideas and tastes, on a spirit of
cooperation and camaraderie, are quite likely to survive the
arrival and departure of sexual interest.

Friendships of the balling-buddy variety are found most
often among marginal social groups who have little investment in conformity. Widespread experimentation along
these lines has been prevalent for some time among the
counterculture: hippies, artists' communities, spiritual
sects, political radicals. Since their deepest commitment is
to something else—a faith, a cause, a life style—these
people understand that they cannot fully commit themselves
to each other. Instead, they offer the loyalty and support
of those bound together by common beliefs and goals: we're
in this together, fighting the system, and we know that
comes first. But we can help each other through the night,
hold each other tight—and in the morning leave each other
free to go about our appointed tasks. Among such groups,
also, role-playing tends to be less rigid. Everyone does his
or her best, whatever is needed for survival.

Various forms of sexual friendship are also being tried
out by large numbers of the separated and divorced—especially the recently divorced. Still nursing their wounds
these people are apt to be gun-shy—understandably wary
of another heavy emotional involvement. At the same time,
they may not want to retreat into a shell; accustomed to
regular doses of love and sex, they may be suffering from
withdrawal and feel acutely miserable and deprived. If
they can find a partner more or less in the same boat, perhaps they can share sex and affection in a way that will not
tax their depleted emotional resources.

Michael McFadden, the bachelor father, says that since
his divorce he has as many women friends as men friends
—something he did not find possible while he was married.

Some of these women are sexual partners, some not; some are former sexual partners or potential sexual partners. There is a fluidity here, for whatever does or does not happen, it is no threat to any existing bond.

Balling buddies are also more likely to be of help with sexual problems, especially those of a temporary nature. The woman who is in love with a man cannot help but take his sexual failings personally; they are seen as affront, rejection, threat, a sign that his love is cooling. She may very well try too hard, or become upset and tearful—in short, her chances of dealing with the difficulty objectively are very slim, though it may have nothing at all to do with her. The man might be demoralized about something else entirely—being out of work, or hating his job, or feeling he's getting old . . . or even the state of the world.

I find it hard to suppress a smile when confronted with the hard-core feminist party line about the sexual habits and behavior of men. Many a guy would be secretly pleased, I am sure, to be considered such a "brute." I think of the thirty-year-old, burned-out rock musician saying, in a voice full of hope and despair, "If you can make me come, you're the Queen of Hearts!" It's the turnabout, all right. A few years ago, it was likely to be the woman who'd go from man to man, looking for the one who would "give" her an orgasm. Now it is often the man who asks the woman to pit her compassion and her erotic energy against the ravages of dissipation, alienation, and despair. *Those* are the difficulties confronting the new non*macho* man. There he is, frightened, yet wanting the powerful goddess to beam that magic ray upon him, excite him, and make him potent in loving again, for only she can bestow upon him the gift of his lost manhood.

Rather than go from woman to woman, the wisest of such men confides his problem to a friend, a woman who isn't in love but is genuinely fond of him. Such a woman friend is able to remove the pressure, for if he doesn't have to perform—if it doesn't matter all that much whether or not he gets it up—half the battle is already won. "Look, nothing is expected of you," said to one nervous young man, worked like a magic incantation. If you can just go to sleep with your arms around each other, he's likely to wake up horny and potent.

The woman, also, may be able to tell a friend what she wants and needs sexually, whereas with the man she adores she might be too shy and nervous, too excited or eager to please. Sexual friendship can be a boon to the New Woman, who knows she's inclined to lose her center, to revert to old roles and outworn patterns, as soon as she becomes "serious" about a man.

Learning to become balling buddies is certainly not "the answer" (surely by now you've stopped looking for "the answer"?), but it *is* one of the more useful of the recipes for survival. Sexual friendship offers an opportunity for learning emotional discipline—it is a retraining ground for developing attitudes and sensibilities more in keeping with our lives and times. Just as women who have learned to be good friends to each other will find it easier to be friends with men, so the feelings and experiences we garner in sexual friendship can be profitably applied to our relations with lovers and spouses.

3
Eros Revisited
or How to Be Your Own...

"Mommy," my daughter asked me when she was about five years old, "what's the 'opposite of sex?'" After I explained her mistake, I continued to ponder the question, which seemed to be quite profound with the addition of the little preposition. The only thing I could think of was ... death.

Sex and death are not really opposed, however, but interrelated in profound and complex ways. They are the two forces which are rooted in nature, the most immutable aspects of our biological destiny—creation and destruction —which we share with all other living creatures. In some species, sex and death coincide; the male dies in the act of copulation. (Even among humans, the male orgasm is sometimes referred to as "the little death.")

Examples of the reciprocity of sex and death abound in literature and legend, as well as in real life. During wars and other disasters, there is usually a marked increase in sexuality and licentiousness—from the poignancy of wartime passion to the almost institutionalized upsurge of

prostitution and rape. By engaging in sexual activity it may
seem as if we are expressing life and warding off death, but
this is not necessarily true. The force which is in true
opposition to death and is genuinely life-affirming is eros—
and that is not at all the same thing as sex. In fact, Dr.
Rollo May, the noted psychotherapist and author, postulates
that sex, in our time, is in direct opposition to eros. Defined
as *desire*, that is, the spirit that infuses us with energy and
enthusiasm, eros is characterized by yearning, longing,
excitement . . . a passionate involvement of one's total being.
While sex seeks release and the reduction of tension, eros
strives for nothing less than union with the beloved—
whatever he or she or it may be. "The essence of eros is that
it draws us from ahead, whereas sex pushes us from behind," is how Dr. May explains the difference, in his book
Love and Will.

One of the great follies of our age is that we confuse the
two, using the terms "sexual" and "erotic" interchangeably.
The ancients, who took sex for granted, never did make
that mistake. Even Freud, toward the end of his career,
felt compelled to distinguish between libido and eros,
against his earlier professed principles. Fully gratified,
libido leads, via the death instinct (Thanatos), to self-
destruction; then eros, the spirit of life, is brought in to
rescue libido from being destroyed by its own self-contradic-
tions.

What this means, in our day and in everyday language, is
that people tend to use sex as a means of evading love, in
any and all its forms. If eros, the universal principle of
loving and relatedness is by-passed in a sexual experience,
the result is sadness and ennui—and eventually, apathy,
the forerunner and harbinger of death. For it is apathy,
not hate, which is the opposite of love. Numbness and
apathy and meaninglessness—those are the symptoms of
the neurotic and schizoid personalities of our times. Our
current obsession with sex—probably unequaled in any
other period of history—thus works as a kind of anesthetic.
It permits us to escape the anxieties of love—and thus of

death, which has come to assume the no-no qualities of obscenity and secretiveness once reserved for sex: you don't talk about it in front of the children, and you try to forget its existence as much as possible.

Eventually, the anesthetic quality extends to the sex itself. We are no longer able to feel anything, only to go through the motions. A sign of how alienated we have become even from our own bodies is that so many people are so willing to turn themselves into fucking machines—the definition of a machine being that it can perform but not feel. The ultimate expression of this strange development is the practice of putting an anesthetic ointment on the head of the penis in order to postpone orgasm. As long as he turns in a good performance, the man doesn't care that he doesn't feel any pleasure. "The computer hovers in the stage wings of the drama of love-making the way Freud said one's parents used to," quips Rollo May.

At the same time, we are becoming more and more aware that there is something amiss. The exiled and repressed eros force drives us on and on, zaps us again and again, causing us to look for the thrill of thrills—the ultimate lay —just over the rainbow. That rage within us, that terrible hunger and craving which seems to seize us with a will of its own, and which we misname sex, is not really for physical release (we can all take care of that by ourselves) but for something else, something much more mysterious and complex.

One woman said what she liked best about sex is the moment when you both know you are going to bed for the first time—that short span of time which is full of excitement and promise, pregnant with possibilities and wonder. After that, she admitted, it was mostly downhill. We do not really dare to open up to the spirit of eros, letting it flow through us freely, for eros has the power to take over our whole being, so that we are no longer completely in control. The eros force is demonic, which means it has the potential for good as well as evil, for destruction as well as creation. Without this force, everything we touch becomes lifeless, yet we still prefer to play it cool—rather safe than sorry. The same woman also said she liked the sense of relief after sex—the smoking of the cigarette and the feeling which she describes thus: "Well, that's that. Got that over with!" So much for *that* promise. Once again, they had teetered on the edge of the precipice and pulled back just in time. Such is the paradox of our modern "free" approach to sex.

Still, there is that terrible craving, and when we find someone to focus it on, it seems dishonest somehow, and smacking of self-punishment, to forgo the opportunity to still the urge, if only for a little while. We are not accustomed, by ideology or training, to by-pass the prospect of immediate pleasure, even in the interests of a possibly greater pleasure in the future. All we have is *now*, goes the rationale. The future scarcely exists; who knows what tomorrow will bring—or if there will *be* a tomorrow. Such a philosophy might well be serviceable if we would really and truly give ourselves over to the Eternal Now. But we don't. Whether we admit it or not, we almost always *are* concerned with the future. If we were not, we would never be afraid to trust—afraid to show too much affection, to experience too much passion, lest it repel or set up too many expectations—lest we or our partner get "hung up."

It is no longer sex we fear, or physical nakedness, but the psychological nakedness of sharing fantasies and dreams, hopes and fears. Without such intimacy, however, sex becomes pretty much like brushing your teeth; small wonder so many young people find it disappointing. Is *that* what everyone made such a big deal about? The kicks their elders used to get from sex they tend to find in drugs, but even these no longer offer the status or the excitement of forbidden adventure they did a few years back. Too much has been told and written about drugs; they are part of a subculture that is on the verge of becoming mainstream (*High Times*, a slick magazine devoted to drug lore, is reputed to have a readership surpassing that of *Playboy*). There seems to be nothing to revolt against anymore—

except sex itself. "The frontier, the establishing of identity, the validation of the self can be, and not infrequently does become for some people, a revolt against sexuality entirely," explains Rollo May. "I am certainly not advocating this," he adds. However, it seems to me that people who have chosen to refrain from sex with others, for a time, are not necessarily giving up—on love or sex. It is more a question of *reculer pour mieux sauter*—pulling back in order to give oneself more room to jump. Sometimes it becomes necessary to break the chain of neurotic repetition, of bed-hoping from partner to partner long after we realize we will never find what we are looking for this way. Before we learn to behave differently, we may have to take a breather and sort things out.

Of the practice of voluntary celibacy, I can only say what has been said of homosexuality and bisexuality: don't knock it if you haven't tried it. First of all, it is important to distinguish between voluntary abstinence and deprivation. This is not a mere semantic distinction but a crucial psychological one. People in a famine starve to death within ten days, whereas people on voluntary fasts have been known to survive over a month. The right state of mind makes all the difference.

Eastern philosophy has gained enough of a foothold in this country for us to comprehend the Oriental concept of the richest person being the one with the fewest needs and desires. The Westerner says, "My cup is half full, let me fill it." The Oriental replies, "My cup is half empty, let me empty it." It seems odd that people who are quite willing and able to go on periodic diets, and even fasts—who will refrain from alcohol or tobacco or marijuana for a time, to clean out the system, reduce the need, or break an addiction to something that has become a necessity rather than a pleasure—are likely to balk at the suggestion that refraining from sex for a while might be beneficial to body and spirit.

Until recent times, the practice of celibacy was highly

regarded not only by religious adepts, whether Christian, Hindu, or Buddhist, but by magicians, mediums, and seers throughout the ages. It is widely believed and documented that the "psi" faculties, or extrasensory perception, are weakened and dissipated by sexual activity. The original intention of celibacy had nothing to do with the concept of sex as sin—and it still doesn't. It is a means, not an end.

At a time when more and more people are hospitable to the practice of yoga and meditation, one wonders why it is so hard to accept the practice of celibacy, which is closely related in history and purpose. In the cultural mishmash of our times, it so happens that the idea of celibacy seems to conflict with the concurrent and highly popular credos of the sexual revolution. But there is really no contradiction. We rightfully crave and demand what is forcibly denied us; once the freedom and the right are ours, we can then decide whether to take it or leave it. (I am reminded of an old joke: The soapbox radical says, "Comes the revolution, you'll eat strawberries and cream." Someone in the audience protests, "But I don't like strawberries and cream." The orator replies, severely, "Comes the revolution, you'll *eat* strawberries and cream.")

People are under the impression that abstaining from sex must be bad for their health. Medical authorities, the popular sexperts, and even such serious reporters as Gail Sheehy, all warn of the dire consequences of sexual inactivity. Men are told they will live longer and remain potent into their dotage if they have sex regularly, and women approaching menopause are given to understand they will "dry up" unless they engage in sex on a steady basis. But if the mucus membranes become thinner with age, having a lot of sex (especially when you're not particularly turned on) can irritate the delicate tissues, causing vaginitis, herpes sores, and other miseries. The general idea is that if you don't keep in practice you will lose it, but I think sex is more like bicycle riding than like ballet: you never forget. My other abstaining friends and I found that, after our period of celibacy, we were able to have sex without any difficulty whatsoever—in fact, we enjoyed it as we had not done in a long time.

If you have been denied sex because of some prohibition, or for lack of opportunity, you are likely to think of nothing else; consequently, you may be climbing the walls within a very short time. Should you, however, get to the point where you are simply not "looking," and you live your life in such a way that the ever-present possibility of sex is not a primary consideration, you may be amazed at the ebbing of tension, at the calm and peace of mind that you might discover. It does not require any dramatic withdrawal, but merely the ability to say to yourself, and mean it: If it happens, O.K., but meanwhile I am going on the assumption that it's not likely to, since I am not seeking or opening to it.

Try to imagine the relief of walking into a room full of people without the more or less subliminal mind-set of "cruising." You look at people in an entirely different way. Men and women you have previously ignored—simply not been aware of because they were not what you'd consider good-looking, say, just not physically attractive to you— may turn out to be interesting, intelligent, amusing people you can thoroughly enjoy. And after getting to know them, you may even find they are really not that bad-looking after all.

As a spectator, temporarily out of the running, you are free to observe couples, and the whole complex mating dance, and what you see with your new perspective can be very instructive indeed. You perceive that sexual tension, or attraction, can be a great deterrent to getting to know another human being. What you see may well serve to reinforce your celibacy which may seem, for the time, the only sane course of action. How deliciously liberating it can be, what a marvelous clear feeling no longer to be what a friend described as "a walking chemistry set, being pulled this way and that by your hormones."

How often have I heard a woman say, "So-and-So is really a neat guy, don't you think, so nice, such a wonderful person," with that peculiar glazed look in the eye which betokens the hormones churning away. And I've looked at the woman in amazement, knowing So-and-So to be a jerk and/or a bastard. Attraction clouds judgment, as we know, and the hormonal derangement can even affect the victim's attitudes toward friends, relatives, and acquaintances, depending on their reaction to the "neat" guy in question. As a rule, the woman has to have an affair with her So-and-So before being able to say, later on, "Whatever did I see in him? I must have been crazy."

Just think: you can fix up your bedroom any way you like instead of doing it part boudoir, and you can keep all sorts of stuff near your bed—reading materials and cosmetics and munchies—for no one is going to be around to comment or pass judgment. As a single woman, you can invite a man to your home for dinner, or an evening of music and drinks, without all the hassles and decisions about going or not going to bed with him. And chances are, when you have explained your feelings, the man will actually be *relieved* (at least that's been my experience—for, dear reader, I would not offer as exotic a recipe for survival as celibacy without having tried it myself). You can explain your position as briefly or elaborately as you like, or however the situation seems to warrant. If you are really sincere, and not playing games, the man will accept it, more often than not, and maybe even be pleased that you invited him for the joy of his company alone. Remember, men have no fewer anxieties about sex than you have, whether they admit it or not.

If a guy doesn't accept it and accuses you of all sorts of horrors, from puritanism to frigidity to dishonesty, you don't want anything to do with him anyway. It is precisely to weed out this kind of man, and the nowhere sexual encounter that you would most likely have with him, that you went on your celibacy trip in the first place. The men may come back or they may not. But they are every bit as likely to come back as if you had gone to bed with them.

Ziva Kwitney, writing in *Ms.*, expresses what many other men and women have told me about their confusions. She wondered how to . . . maneuver in that mating dance that is at the core of contemporary "dating" relationships. How should I respond to sexual advances when I was interested, but had doubts? What was the best way to say no when I wasn't attracted to the man, but didn't want to hurt his feelings? . . . What should I do when I had sex with a man and didn't want to again? And, God help me, what did I do with my bruised psyche when it was the other way around? It all seemed to boil down to expectations, his of me, and mine of him, before, during and after. And it all seemed equally treacherous: one of us invariably expected more than there was and was let down. Or worse yet, having engaged in the most intimate physical encounter there is, I would end up feeling *more* distant, *more* alone, less loved and less loving than before.

Several men I talked with who admitted having been celibate for some time—as long as a year, in one case—attributed it to their unwillingness, or inability, to play the hunting game. Somehow, their hearts were no longer in it; they had lost their taste for the chase. The implication was always that they were open—if only the right woman would come along and "seduce" them, all would be well. But, as we have seen, they are probably deluding themselves in this regard.

Being celibate does not necessarily mean doing without sex altogether, at least not in the present context. True, quite a few people who have no inhibitions about social sex still feel guilty about masturbation. However, "workshops" which purport to "teach" women how to masturbate, like the much-publicized one taught by Betty Dodson, a painter turned sex therapist, somehow beg the question. It is not really a matter of technique, but of feeling free to do it *when you are alone*. That's the whole point, the comfort and consolation of masturbation. By doing it in a group, within a "therapeutic" framework, you are changing the nature of the act, which is in essence, a solitary one. What goes on in those classes is closer to the "touchie-feelie" type of psychological encounter games. While it may free some women to do it by themselves, it may hinder others from understanding that the real value of masturbation lies in the fact that there *is* no audience—you can be completely yourself.

Even if you have no compunctions about pleasuring yourself, you may find, after you have been celibate for a while, that you do not feel like masturbating anywhere near as much as you supposed you would. A lot of the time, it simply does not seem worth the effort. "You masturbate and you masturbate, and then one day it leaves your life," said Renata. "Because that's not what life is about." This odd development, reported by a number of celibates, would indicate to me that the purely physical need might be greatly exaggerated. Perhaps people actually enjoy the low-level sexual tension which, according to Ms. Kwitney, has a vitality and excitement of its own. "Oddly, it was a very sexual period for me," she explained. "I became sensitive to my body, to its contours and rhythms and textures."

Another, perhaps more interesting, way to experience sexual release is in dreams. The perfecting of erotic dreams, to the heights of satisfaction and actual orgasm, is a task that might occupy the conscientious student of dream control for many happy nights. Patricia Garfield, in her book, *Creative Dreaming,* claims it is possible to achieve total release in dreams and suggests specific ways to accomplish this, as well as other ways to make our dreams more rewarding. Most of her methods involve suggestions while awake—rather along the lines of selfhypnotic suggestions. Such techniques have been used for centuries by yogis and other mental adepts. Garfield feels it is not only pleasurable but also beneficial to attempt to program our dreams. The aim is to lessen the gap between conscious and unconscious, to bring our inner and outer worlds into harmony, and the connecting lines go both ways.

Looking forward to one's dreams ... knowing one may wake at any hour of the night and turn on the light to jot down a dream, or merely to savor it, can be one of the sweetest aspects of sleeping alone. This exciting "night life" not only provides positive feedback to waking life, making you feel more energetic, in a calm sort of way, but it can also provide valuable insight into what type of persons, and what kind of situations, really turn you on.

People have told me that, during their periods of celibacy, they felt the same heightened awareness they experienced during a fast. "My celibacy was for me a body-and-mind meditation," wrote Ms. Kwitney.

> It made me peaceful, it made me stronger, it expanded my sense of myself as *myself*. ... I began to have a sense of myself as a universe, complete, without need of another. Even my desire, when it came, was my own—to contain as a pleasure, or to satisfy by my own hand. "I'm the woman in charge around here," I would think to myself.

Thus it would seem, paradoxically, that celibacy can be a way of learning to love oneself. If people are repelled by this idea, it may be that they mistakenly equate self-love with selfishness. Before we can love others, however, we must love ourselves—the mind healers have been telling us this for decades, but we still don't quite believe it. If we don't love ourselves, we are unable to *accept* love, convinced we are unworthy—or else we turn greedy and demanding in a fruitless attempt to fill our own emptiness with the attentions and favors of others.

Of course, the period of celibacy will probably not last. It isn't *meant* to last. Sooner or later, something in your life will change—you will meet someone, and marvel once again at the magic of touch, the miracle of the sexual connection, and wonder how you managed to do so long without. In the meantime, however, you will have simplified your life—cleaned out a system that has become jaded and turned off by too much indulgence, too much frustration and disappointment. After a year and a half of celibacy, Ziva Kwitney meets a man with whom she is willing and able to try "the scary journey back" (my own celibacy trip lasted eight months).

She finds (as I d_d) that somehow her attitude and approach are differen:. She is able to enjoy sex again. But she knows she will periodically return to celibacy,

> to get back to that territory where I am total center. I see that there is some work on the self that can only be done alone, independent of relationships. That work is the affirmation of oneself. *You are the only one who will never leave you,* someone once told me. Curiously, it is a thought that reassures me.

Celibacy can be one way of relearning what loving is all about. Loving not as a task to be worked at, nor as an art to be perfected, nor as gratification of ego, but loving as *union*—a reaching out and opening up to the cosmic creative forces, the original power source, the driving motor of the universe. According to no lesser an authority than Saint Augustine, eros is the force that moves man toward God. Eros is also the force that drives man toward knowledge, toward ethical truth—"the knowledge of good and evil"—according to Plato, the Greek dramatists, as well as the authors of Genesis. Adam and Eve, Oedipus Rex, *had* to find out, even if the knowledge would destroy them, even though they were forewarned. For truth is one aspect of the deity we are forever yearning toward. The seemingly curious juxtaposition of sex and knowledge in both these myths points up the dangerous aspects of the eros striving: the truth may set you free, but it may also destroy you. Icarus, driven by eros passion to transcend his limitations, flew too high and was burned by the sun—a myth that seems to have profound meaning for our times. For eros drives the inventor and the explorer, as well as the poet and the seer—all those who lust after knowledge and truth, who are forever seeking to expand and create new forms.

Eros is the power that causes us to love "not wisely but too well"—not for what's in it for us, but for the sake of loving itself. Such love may not have much to do with the objective merits of the beloved. The phrase "that only a mother could love" describes precisely this quality of loving, which is independent of the attributes of the loved one. In fact, the recipient of such love might want no part of it —the passion and intensity of the lover might even frighten and repel, when there is no answering passion. But the lover, though suffering from rejection, is in the grip of something beyond such considerations as whether or not the love is returned.

The lover might be better off if the passion *is* unrequited. At least one can go on with everyday life, writing one's poems, as Dante did for Beatrice. It is mutual passion which is the most dangerous: two fires are apt to consume themselves, as well as those around them. Fortunately perhaps, mutual passion of great intensity is very rare. Such love is like a force of nature, transforming everything in its wake. It is the intuition that mysterious, cosmic forces are tapped that accounts for our enduring fascination with the great lovers of history and legend. Helen and Paris, Antony and Cleopatra, Heloise and Abelard—what did these lovers have to do with "relationships"?—they set in motion cataclysmic forces, and were themselves undone.

Needless to say, the eros force varies greatly, in intensity as well as intent, depending on our temperaments and the way we handle it. Whether we are controlled by eros or are able to work *with* it. in full consciousness, makes the difference between creation and destruction, which may be balanced by no more than a hair. It seems easier to flow with the eros love when it involves something transhuman —an ideal, a discovery, an artistic creation. But even here, the nether side of eros cannot always be evaded. One has only to think of the many saints martyred, revolutionaries executed, and poets suicided, to realize that such "pure" love does not exempt one from "punishment"—that is, from having to pay the ultimate prices, madness and death, for the privilege of experiencing so powerful and life-enhancing a passion.

Most of us, however, are neither mystics nor great artists. Ordinary human beings tap into the eros force either individually, through love of other human beings, or collectively, via religious ritual and political affiliation. In our

day, however, religion and politics are no longer good "con-
ductors" for this force. Churches and shrines have pretty
much ceased to be power stations where eros energy could
be stored and accumulated and connected with. People
who take their religion too seriously are looked at askance,
as "weirdos," and patriotism has become practically a dirty
word.

But we cannot suppress the passional springs of life forever; one way or the other, eros will not be denied. More
than likely, eros will out in its most primitive and destructive form, which is violence. Paradoxically, violence both
real and vicarious has come to be what makes a lot of people
feel most alive—what permits them to experience to any
degree that excitement, that current of energy characteristic of the eros force. Violence in our time will not abate
until we rediscover ways to integrate eros into our daily
lives in a constructive and meaningful fashion.

Where there is a need, there is a way. The widespread
interest in psychotherapy is one attempt to deal with eros
by exploring the unconscious, which is the vehicle by which
eros moves. As misguided as this interest sometimes can
be, it is nevertheless a step in the right direction, and so
are the experiments, albeit dangerous, with mind-expanding
drugs. Other ways of reaffirming eros include the renewed
interest in spirituality and religion, and the renewed fascination with occult and psychic phenomena and various
other methods of exploring what goes on in outer, as well
as inner, space.

Our current obsession with sex, as well as the inordinate
emphasis we place on individual, romantic love bonds are
signs of the paucity of outlets for the pent-up eros energy.
When we have truly grasped that love in its larger creative
sense must inform a greater proportion of our lives, we
may then be able to put sex and love into proper perspective.

Aside from eros, the principle of creation and procreation, and *philia*, the friendship love of peers, there is still

another kind of love, which the Greeks called *agape*. The Buddhists call it compassion, the Christians mercy. The spirit of eros involves reaching out and striving toward— the spirit of *agape* means opening up and taking in. One is yang, the other yin; they are, respectively, *Chien*, the Creative, and *Kun*, the Receptive, as described in the first two hexagrams of the *I Ching*. *Agape* without eros becomes a sterile nirvana of contemplating one's navel, and it was insufficient eros that weakened the "otherworldy" faiths of Hinduism, Buddhism, and certain forms of Christianity. And it is insufficient *agape* that drives our eros-sickened age into violence and the creation of life-destroying forms, such as the atomic bomb.

Toward our fellow humans and toward ourselves, also, eros must be tempered with *agape*, as well as with *philia*, if it is to achieve harmony and balance. As we have seen, eros alone can be very destructive. Eros is the force which repels as well as attracts, and it is for this reason that love so often appears in tragic guise. "The smallest molecular particle gets its dynamic movement from the fact that it consists of a positive and negative charge, with tension— and therefore movement—between them," writes Rollo May. He goes on to explain that this touch and withdrawal, what zoologists call the "approach-avoidance" syndrome, is present even in the hesitant beginnings of acquaintance-ship and constitutes the essence of courtship, in animals as well as humans.

It is important for us to understand that the two com-plementary needs, to unite and to separate, are inextricably interwoven in the fabric of love. The ideal of "togetherness" is untenable, and ambivalence toward our loved ones is not to be avoided. That's what the poignancy of love, the joy and sorrow of it, are all about. We yearn for union, but as soon as we have joined with our loved ones, we must separate again—or else, we will be destroyed. This is the lesson and the moral of all the tales and myths about love.

It is in this context that love of self, properly understood, can be most productive. We do not always want to be alone, no more than we always want to be with others—we need distance from ourselves, as from others we love. But love of self means we *can* enjoy ourselves alone; we can appreciate the moonlit night and starry sky, and be uplifted by it, without our pleasure being marred, or turned to sorrow by the thought: "Where is the lover to share this night with me?" All too often, we fail to savor the good things life does have to offer—the beauties of nature, music, fine food—because we cannot accept pleasure that is not shared; it is somehow shameful to enjoy a moonlit night by ourselves.

There is a universal tendency for the eros force to degenerate and become merely sex. This is precisely what has happened in our time. The ancient Greeks already knew of this tendency. In the original legend, Eros was a vigorous youth whose arrow, shot into the earth, caused her to burst forth with green. Later on, as Greek civilization grew more effete, Eros became a mischievous child, irresponsible, and *blindfolded* to boot. The latter myth tells us that Eros did not grow like other children but remained a chubby infant. Alarmed for his health, his mother, Aphrodite, consulted the oracle, which replied, "Love cannot grow without passion."

Understanding these deeper dimensions enables us to approach the sexual wilderness with new eyes, so that we can establish guideposts based on something other than the current, popular shibboleths of our times. In a way, we have to start from scratch. "There is a lag between the end of an age and the discovery of the end," says Walker Percy, in *The Message in the Bottle*.

> The denizens of such a time are like the cartoon cat that runs off a cliff and for a while is suspended, still running, in mid-air but sooner or later looks down and sees there is nothing under him.

We no longer understand ourselves because the theories of the former age no longer work, and the theories of the

new age are not yet known—for not even the *fact* of the
new age is known. And so everything is confused, people
feeling bad when they should feel good, and good when
they should feel bad; sad when they make love, and energized when they are violent and destructive.

One of the basics we need to rediscover is the simple
joy of human companionship. Anyone who has seen the
look of rapture on the face of a child who has found a new
friend can never again doubt that this is love in its essence:
the feeling of just wanting to *be* with someone—of feeling
energized, *high,* when in the presence of this particular
person. It is even possible to feel the charge at a distance.
Talking on the phone, or writing letters, or even just *thinking* about the one we love can give us that feeling of well-
being, of making life seem worth living. When we apply
this simple criterion to our various "relationships," we
might just find that we love best those whom we appreciate
least, those whose love we take for granted. We might feel
that way about a friend, or a relative, or someone we've
just met. And we may let these people go, without a qualm,
unaware that love has just passed us by. This will happen
less as we learn to reaffirm the many dimensions of love
which we now ignore or devalue—including a healthy dose
of self-love.

"*L'amour est tellement simple,*" says the heroine of the
French film classic, *Les Enfants du Paradis.* But the sim-
plest things are often the most difficult to attain.

The difficulties should not deter us, however. For this
transitional age is a time of opportunity—of new possibilities and alternatives. In the process of dealing with our
individual crises, we are often able to discover new mean-
ings and dimensions to the problems of humanity. We may
realize that consciousness, mankind's most outstanding
characteristic, allows us to influence our destiny at least
to some extent. By throwing our weight behind one tendency rather than another—by realizing that habits and
patterns *can* be changed—we participate in our own development, as well as that of the society we live in, and give
some meaning to the ideas of freedom and responsibility.

Far from wanting merely to preserve their own existence and to survive at all costs, human beings have a strange propensity to strive for more, to enhance themselves. Even the most primitive societies practiced their rituals and magic in order to grow and learn, to generate more life. And in their striving effort, individuals are often willing to risk their own lives.

Seen in this light, our dissatisfactions and our pain need not be in vain, for we can take the opportunity to surpass our present limitations. Pain is a warning signal, the reaction of a healthy organism to an unhealthy condition. In these pessimistic and deterministic times, it is important to remember that we have gone through many changes and will go through many more, and that in the evolutionary scheme of things, those who are not destroyed by their struggles emerge from them stronger than ever.

Bibliography

BOOKS

BARNES, DJUNA. *Nightwood.* New York: New Directions, 1946.

BENGIS, INGRID. *Combat in the Erogenous Zone.* New York: Alfred A. Knopf, 1953.

BERNARD, JESSIE. *The Sex Game: Communication Between the Sexes.* New York: Atheneum, 1972.

———. *Remarriage: A Study of Marriage.* New York: Russell & Russell, 1971.

CAMPBELL, JOSEPH. *The Masks of God: Primitive Mythology.* New York: Viking Press, 1959.

CHARNY, ISRAEL. *Marital Love and Hate.* New York: Macmillan Publishing Co., 1972.

DE BEAUVOIR, SIMONE. *The Second Sex.* New York: Alfred A. Knopf, 1953.

DIDION, JOAN. *Slouching Towards Bethlehem.* New York: Farrar, Straus & Giroux, 1968.

FISHER, SEYMOUR. *The Female Orgasm.* New York: Basic Books, 1972.

GARFIELD, PATRICIA. *Creative Dreaming.* New York: Simon & Schuster, 1975.

GILDER, GEORGE. *Naked Nomads: Unmarried Men in America.* New York: Quadrangle/The New York Times Co., 1974.

———. *Sexual Suicide.* New York: Quadrangle/The New York Times Co., 1973.

GOODMAN, PAUL. *Growing Up Absurd.* New York: Random House, 1960.

GREER, GERMAINE. *The Female Eunuch.* New York: McGraw-Hill Book Co., 1971.

HARDING, M. ESTHER. *Psychic Energy: Its Source and Goal.* New York: Pantheon Books (Bollingen Foundation), 1950.

———. *The Way of All Women.* New York: G. P. Putnam's Sons (C. G. Jung Foundation for Analytical Psychology), 1970.

HART, HAROLD H., ed. *Marriage: For and Against.* New York: Hart Publishing Co., 1972.

JANEWAY, ELIZABETH. *Between Myth and Morning: Women Awakening.* New York: William Morrow & Co., 1974.

———. *Man's World, Woman's Place: A Study in Social Mythology.* New York: William Morrow & Co., 1971.

JOURARD, SIDNEY M. *The Transparent Self: Self-Disclosure and Well-Being.* New York: Van Nostrand Reinhold Co., 1971.

JUNG, CARL GUSTAV. *Collected Works.* Vol. 13. *Alchemical Studies.* G. Adler, *et al.*, eds. New York: Pantheon Books, 1950.

KINSEY, ALFRED C., *et al. Sexual Behavior in the Human Female.* Philadelphia: W. B. Saunders Co., 1953.

LESSING, DORIS. *The Golden Notebook.* New York: Simon & Schuster, 1962.

———. *The Summer Before the Dark.* New York: Alfred A. Knopf, 1973.

———. *The Temptation of Jack Orkney.* New York: Alfred A. Knopf, 1973.

LORENZ, KONRAD. *On Aggression.* New York: Harcourt Brace Jovanovich, 1966.

LUNDBERG, FERDINAND, and FARNHAM, MARYNIA F. *Modern Woman: The Lost Sex.* New York: Grosset & Dunlap, 1947.

MCFADDEN, MICHAEL. *Bachelor Fatherhood: How to Raise and Enjoy Your Children As a Single Parent.* New York: Walker & Co., 1974.

MAILER, NORMAN. *The Prisoner of Sex.* Boston: Little, Brown & Co., 1971.

MASTERS, WILLIAM H., and JOHNSON, VIRGINIA E. *Human Sexual Response.* Boston: Little, Brown & Co., 1966.

———. *The Pleasure Bond: A New Look at Sexuality and Commitment.* Boston: Little, Brown & Co., 1975.

MAY, ROLLO. *Love and Will.* New York: W. W. Norton & Co., 1969.

NIN, ANAÏS. *The Diary of Anaïs Nin,* Vol. I. 1931–34. Gunther Stuhl-
mann, ed. New York: Harcourt, Brace & World, 1966.

O'NEILL, NENA, and O'NEILL, GEORGE. *Open Marriage: A New Life
Style for Couples.* New York: M. Evans, 1972.

PERCY, WALKER. *The Message in the Bottle.* New York: Farrar,
Straus & Giroux, 1975.

PLATH, SYLVIA. *The Bell Jar.* New York: Harper & Row, 1971.

REUBEN DAVID. *Any Woman Can.* New York: Bantam, 1972.

————. *Everything You Always Wanted to Know About Sex and
Were Afraid to Ask.* New York: David McKay Co., Inc., 1969.

ROGERS, CARL R. *Becoming Partners: Marriage and Its Alternatives.*
New York: Delacorte Press, 1972.

SARTON, MAY. *Journal of a Solitude.* New York: W. W. Norton & Co.,
1973.

SHEEHY, GAIL. *Passages.* New York: E. P. Dutton & Co., 1976.

STEIN, MARTHA L. *Lovers, Friends, Slaves . . . The Nine Male Sexual
Types.* New York: Berkley Publishing Corp. and G. P. Putnam's
Sons, 1974.

STEPHENS, JAMES. *The Crock of Gold.* New York: Macmillan Publishing Co., 1960.

VASSI, MARCO. *The Saline Solution.* New York: Olympia Press, 1971.

VILAR, ESTHER. *The Manipulated Man.* New York: Farrar, Straus &
Giroux, 1972.

WEISS, MICHAEL. *Living Together: A Year in the Life of a City
Commune.* New York: McGraw-Hill Book Co., 1974.

WELDON, FAY. *Female Friends.* New York: St. Martin's Press, 1974.

WILSON, COLIN. *The Sex Diaries of Gerard Sorme.* New York: Dial
Press, 1963.

WILSON, EDWARD O. *Sociobiology: The New Synthesis.* Cambridge,
Mass.: Belknap/Harvard University Press, 1975.

ARTICLES

JULTY, SOLOMON "SAM." "Men: A Case of Erective Dysfunction,"
Ms., Oct. 1972.

NOBILE, PHILIP. "What Is the New Impotence, and Who's Got It?"
Esquire, Oct. 1972.

SELIG, ELAINE BOOTH, BOUCHER, SANDY, and KWITNEY, ZIVA. "Living
Without Them—Three Who Tried It and Like It," *Ms.,* Oct. 1975.

About the Author

Uta West grew up in New York City. She received her B.A. from Brooklyn College, did graduate work at Columbia University, and has taught at Denver University and the College of the Virgin Islands. Ms. West is the author of three novels and a number of articles, which have appeared in *Viva, Penthouse, Pageant, Countdown,* and other publications. Her most recent book is an anthology, *Women in a Changing World.* She lives on Cape Cod with her eleven-year-old daughter.